WINGS
OVER THE
DESERT

Rejected as unfit, Eric Seward learned to fly privately, intending to join his cousins in France's Aéronautique Militaire. Here he is in September 1915 at Hall's Flying School, Hendon, after his first solo flight. (Author's collection)

WINGS
OVER THE
DESERT

In action with an RFC pilot in Palestine 1916–18

Desmond Seward

Haynes Publishing

First published in 2009

A catalogue record for this book is available from the British Library

ISBN 978 1 84425 672 3

Library of Congress control no. 2009929520

Published by Haynes Publishing, Sparkford, Yeovil, Somerset BA22 7JJ, UK
Tel: 01963 442030 Fax: 01963 440001
Int. tel: +44 1963 442030 Int. fax: +44 1963 440001
E-mail: sales@haynes.co.uk
Website: www.haynes.co.uk

Haynes North America Inc.
861 Lawrence Drive, Newbury Park,
California 91320, USA

Printed and bound in Great Britain

CONTENTS

For Aymeri and Cecilia de Montalembert

ACKNOWLEDGEMENTS

This is a book about my father, William Eric Louis Seward, a portrait of one man and his war. Half memoir, half chronicle, it describes his First World War experiences – sometimes exhilarating, often terrifying, and which scarred him for life. The book began as notes to accompany the photograph albums and negatives found many years after he died, which I only recently discovered could be restored. In trying to write about what he saw and felt, however, I realized that it would be impossible to do so without giving an overall picture of the Palestine Front. The result has no pretensions to being a definitive history, but merely sets an ordinary pilot's story in context.

The 'Great War' has now become as distant as the Peninsular War was in Edwardian times. Even so, what I was told by one man about his small part in it remains so clearly in my mind that it still seems to me as if it had happened only yesterday, and I feel that it would be a shame were it all to be forgotten. Although a good deal of his behaviour and prejudices may perhaps upset some of today's readers – he was very much a man of his age – I have decided that it is best to give an unvarnished picture.

During the First World War Britain's campaign against the Ottoman Empire culminated at Megiddo in autumn 1918 when General Sir Edmund Allenby destroyed all three Turkish armies opposing him. If less massive a conflict than on the Western Front, in some ways it was more dramatic, since it was the last cavalry war. The future Field Marshal Wavell, who was there, described the earlier phases as 'marches and battles across the scorching sands of the Sinai Desert, combat in the rocky hills north of Beersheba, the waterless pursuit after the fall of Gaza, close-range-fighting among the orange-groves south of Jaffa'.[1] The later phases, in the Judaean Hills and then east of the Jordan, ended with the whirlwind capture of Nazareth and Damascus. The best-known aspect is, of course, T. E. Lawrence and his Arab revolt.

Yet, apart from the official history, *The War in the Air*, and a few lines in Lawrence's *Seven Pillars of Wisdom*, little has been published about the Royal Flying Corps' role. Without the help of the RFC – or, later, the RAF – Allenby could never have won his victories. One reason why almost nothing has been written about his pilots is that there were so few of them. As late as mid-1917, the RFC seldom had more than 20 serviceable machines to send into action on the Palestine Front, in contrast to the hundreds in France. Until 1918 there were far fewer 'dogfights', and none of those aces whose exploits in France became such a tonic for the Home Front.

This book looks at the campaign from the RFC's point of view, especially from that of members of 5th Wing, which was made of two squadrons – the RFC's No. 14 and the Australian Flying Corps' No. 1. It re-creates what it was like being a pilot in the Sinai Desert, in the Gaza area and in the Judaean Hills during the war with Turkey and the Central Powers. As far as possible, it is built around my father (with No. 14 Squadron during 1916 and 1917 and then with the School of Aeronautics at Heliopolis), whose outlook and way of speaking I have tried to recapture.

As has been said, the primary inspiration is his photographs, but he left some useful letters, while No. 14 Squadron's war diary (*recte*, 'Operations Record Book, No. 14 (Bombing) Squadron') from the National Archives at Kew has been an enormous help. Not the original diary – jotted down each day in 'indelible pencil' – this is a rewritten copy, typed out at the end of the war. (A manuscript note at the end says that the squadron was disbanded on 4 February 1919.) I have been unable to discover the identity of the author or authors, but he or they must have been members of the squadron since such pride has been taken in it. Although the writing is clumsy, it somehow manages to strike a valedictory, even an elegiac, note. In addition, among my father's papers I found several issues of *The Gnome* for 1917, a little magazine for the RFC in the Middle East, never more than 20 pages long, published every two months, which was edited by Captain J. E. Dixon-Spain. His editorials and the articles have been invaluable in trying to understand the men who flew on the Palestine Front. (Probably fewer than a hundred copies of each issue were printed – it is not in the library of the Imperial War Museum.)

Plenty of information is available about the other half of 5th Wing, No. 1 Squadron, Australian Flying Corps, from the history of the AFC during the war that was published by Frederick Cutlack in 1923, based on its war diary or

Cover of The Gnome *(named after the engine of so many early planes), a magazine for the RFC on the Sinai Front that was edited by Captain J. E. Dixon-Spain while on active service with No. 14 Squadron.* (Author's collection)

on information from members of the squadron. Forerunners of their country's air force, understandably they arouse a great deal of interest in Australia. But because my book is built around my father and No. 14 Squadron, I have not gone into detail about them.

Above all, there are the tales told to me by my father. I was fairly close to him and he was one of the best raconteurs I have ever met. I remember vividly his accounts of aerial dogfights and how to deal with a Fokker *Eindecker* when it dived on you out of the sun, of how to evade machine-gun bursts from a pursuing enemy, of what it felt like to be shot down without a parachute, of a missed chance of killing the enemy commander, of meeting T. E. Lawrence. (No. 14 was the squadron that went to Lawrence's help.) He described the fighting qualities of such German machines as the 'bull-nosed' Albatros or the Halberstadt, saying how much he admired the gallantry of the Kaiser's airmen, whom he was always trying to kill – and who were always trying to kill him. He also mentioned the strange code of chivalry that existed between them.

They flew without parachutes ('bad for morale') but which in any case could not be packed into a tiny cockpit. In consequence, to be shot down often meant incineration. When a machine burst into flames in mid-air, the pilot would frequently throw himself out and fall thousands of feet to his death, to avoid being burned alive.

My father was lucky to survive. The dust jacket of this volume features a copy of a painting called *The Seward Exploit*, which hung in the Imperial War Museum until 1939 (when it made way for Second World War trophies) and shows him escaping from Turkish cavalry after his plane had been brought down in the sea by shell-fire. In any case, for those who flew them, the period's aircraft were as much a danger as enemy action. He had five other major crashes, smashing his already broken nose twice more so that it was literally flattened. After just over a year of front-line service, even his strong nerves cracked and he was grounded by a succession of medical boards. Years later, the mental damage he suffered would cause a complete collapse.

I wish to thank the National Archives at Kew, the British Library, the London Library and the Imperial War Museum – notably the Department of Printed Books and Documents, and the Department of Art where Sarah Bevan was exceptionally helpful. I must also thank Philip Jarrett for letting me use some of his own archive of photographs. I am particularly grateful to James Drummond-Murray for doing so much invaluable research and tracking down the war diary of No. 14 Squadron. I owe a great deal to Sir John Hervey-

Certificate No. 1642.

ROYAL FLYING CORPS.

(Officers.)

CENTRAL FLYING SCHOOL,

UPAVON, WILTS.,

6th July 1916.

GRADUATION CERTIFICATE.

THIS IS TO CERTIFY that *2nd Lieut W E S Seward,*

Royal Flying Corps (S.R)

has completed a *~~long~~* *in the military Wing.* course ~~at the Central Flying School~~, and is qualified

~~short~~

for service in the Royal Flying Corps.

a.e. mac lean

Lieut. Col.
Commandant.

* Strike out word not applicable.

W 8197—3244   500   8/15   H W V(P 1163/2)   H. 16/829
1916—7221   1000   5/16

WELS's official flying certificate from the RFC. (Author's collection)

Bathurst, for reading the typescript and providing some brutally frank but extremely useful criticisms.

I had the good fortune to meet Allen Sangines-Krause, who told me of what he heard from his grandfather about the other side's experience on the Palestine Front. An officer of Prinz Eugen of Savoy's Dragoons in the Austro-Hungarian Army, Rittmeister Albrecht Krause was attached to General von Falkenhayn's Staff, and left the only surviving account of the RFC's 'Bully Beef Raid' at the Third Battle of Gaza.

I am also most grateful to my very professional editors, Jonathan Falconer and Alison Miles, and to my incomparable agent, Andrew Lownie.

Finally, I should like to thank Stella Lesser for all her hard work in reading the proofs.

Notes

1. Lord Wavell, *Allenby: Soldier and Statesman*, p. 143.

'HUN CHIVALRY'

'In some areas the World War was conducted with good manners, by people who had been well brought up – I might almost go so far as to say that it was a gentleman's war.'

Jean Renoir, note to **La Grande Illusion**

At sunrise on 5 March 1917 all the aircraft of No. 14 Squadron still in working order took off from an aerodrome at Ujret el Zol near El Arish in the Sinai Desert – known to the RFC as 'Kilo 143'. Comprising half of Colonel A. E. Borton's 5th Wing, they formed a motley collection, which included six two-seater BE2Cs and a lone two-seater 'pusher', a De Havilland DH1, together with three single-seater Martinsyde 'Elephants' and two single-seater Bristol Scouts. Among the Martinsyde pilots was a 25-year-old, red-headed 'Franco-Irishman' with a broken nose, Eric Seward, who had joined the squadron during the previous summer.

This was an unusually big reconnaissance patrol, its mission to investigate the Turkish lines around Gaza. The information was urgently needed for Major-General Sir Archibald Murray's imminent offensive to end Turkey's threat to the Suez Canal. The BE2Cs' job was to photograph the enemy artillery. The single-seaters and the 'pusher' were there to defend them from attack by Fliegerabteilung 300 of the Luftstreitkräfte (the name given to the German Army's recently reorganised air force), which was operating from aerodromes at Beersheba and Ramleh.

The airmen had risen from their camp-beds before dawn, some already woken by the cold, but the sun rose so swiftly that by the time they climbed into their aircraft it was oppressively hot, and when they set off from Kilo 143 they were grateful for the cooler world of the clouds. It soon became too cold again, however, in their open cockpits, since they flew without protective clothing. Yet despite the cold – and the deafening noise from their engines and the wind – they had more to think about than the temperature.

Everyone knew that the BE2Cs were dangerously vulnerable – on the Western Front they were nicknamed 'Fokker Fodder'. The Jumbo Martinsydes (or 'Tin-sides') were a bit faster, but their top speed was only 87 mph. Like the tiny little Bristol Scouts, each was armed with a Lewis gun mounted on the centre section of the upper wing, firing outside the radius of the propeller.

An attempt to intercept the flight by a handful of German scouts was driven off, even if the enemy had started to supplement their Aviatiks and Fokker monoplanes with 'bull-nosed' Albatros DIIIs and Halberstadts that were technically six months in advance of the local RFC planes. Not only faster, German aircraft were armed with machine guns that had 'interrupter' gear enabling them to fire through the propeller arc. Luckily for the British, they amounted to no more than a squadron, less than the normal 'Jasta' on the Western Front, and today only a few were in evidence. Nor does 'Archie' fire from the enemy's anti-aircraft guns seem to have been particularly effective on this occasion. When the mission was completed, which was fairly soon since their planes had a very limited range, No. 14 Squadron turned back for home and breakfast.

After landing, they were horrified to learn that one of the BE2Cs, piloted by Lieutenant Floyer with 2nd Lieutenant Palmer as observer, had failed to return. If shot down, they might have burned to cinders (since the RFC flew without parachutes); if they had made a forced landing, they would die from thirst or perhaps be tortured to death by Bedouin. Everyone knew they themselves might go the same way. T. E. Lawrence, who saw a lot of them, realized that airmen were bundles of nerves – like his Arabs, they 'lived for the day and died for it'.[1] A plane set off to search for Floyer and Palmer, but found nothing. The Colonel suggested that everybody have 'a damn good lunch', which was code for drown their sorrows in drink.

Three days later, on the morning of 8 March, while the only six machines of No. 14 Squadron now serviceable were out bombing Junction Station, north of Arak el Menshiye, a two-seater Rumpler dived down from 4,000 ft over the landing ground at Kilo 143 and dropped a 'smoke ball', followed by a message bag. Then it flew off. Because this was mistaken for a bombing attack, two Australian aircraft from No. 1 Squadron, which was also based at El Arish, took off to attack the Rumpler, but it was too fast for them.

The message was a letter from the Germans, saying they regretted having to inform their British opponents that they had shot down one of their machines. Luckily, however, pilot and observer had survived to enjoy an excellent lunch in their mess. The bag also contained requests from Floyer

*'Hun Chivalry'. Fliegerabteilung 300 with Lieutenant Floyer and 2nd Lieutenant Palmer
of No. 14 Squadron, whom they have just shot down and entertained to 'a damn good
lunch' at Beersheba Aerodrome on 5 March 1917. At the Germans' invitation their
pyjamas and shaving kit were dropped on the mess at Beersheba. Oberleutnant Gerhard
Felmy is marked '1' and Leutnant Richard Falke '2'. Note the two Austro-Hungarian
pilots, front left and behind Felmy. Both sides treated captured air crew like this, but the
'Huns' began the custom. From* The Gnome, May 1917. (Author's collection)

and Palmer for pyjamas and shaving tackle, with a note from their captors
promising that these might be delivered in safety. That afternoon, a British
aircraft dropped the items at Beersheba, with a message of thanks and also
an apology from the Australians for trying to intercept the Rumpler. German
fliers, some in white tropical uniform, stood outside their mess waving up
at the pilot.

On 18 March another enemy aeroplane visited Kilo 143. Again, the pilot
signalled with a smoke bomb, shut off his engine, came down to 1,000 ft and
then dropped a satchel. This contained a photograph of Floyer and Palmer

surrounded by German officers, including Gerhard Felmy and Richard Falke, the two fliers who had delivered the first message. With them were two Austro-Hungarian pilots.[2]

In addition, there was a letter from the German commander, Hauptmann Hellmuth Felmy (Gerhard's brother), to say that No. 14 Squadron's machines were always welcome to deliver messages and prisoners' kit; he gave his word that the German artillery would be ordered not to fire on British aeroplanes so long as they followed an agreed course at 1,000 metres and signalled with a smoke ball over a specified point. He also invited everybody at Kilo 143 to stay with him at his house in the country in Pomerellen, 'as soon as this boring war is over'.

A British pilot dropped a reply on the enemy aerodrome, politely declining the offer. This chilly response can be explained by the British Army's fear that any form of fraternization might weaken morale and the determination to destroy the enemy at all costs – no doubt a legacy of the famous 'Christmas Truce' of 1914 in Flanders. Yet the incident made a lasting impression on RFC pilots in Palestine, who began to see German fliers as human beings. Despite the prohibition, contact was discreetly maintained while, in the rare event of any enemies surviving after being shot down, they were invited to lunch and plied with champagne. On one occasion, the welcome was misunderstood by a Turkish observer,[3] who looked noticeably glum throughout the meal, refusing to cheer up – only later did his hosts learn that he had expected to be tortured as soon as they finished eating.[4]

I used to wonder if my father's memories of 'Hun chivalry' were exaggerated or wishful thinking. But, quite recently, I found among his papers a copy of the May 1917 issue of *The Gnome*. It contains a full account of the incident, together with a photograph of Floyer and Palmer surrounded by their captors at Beersheba.[5]

The opening scenes of Jean Renoir's film of 1937, *La Grande Illusion*, re-create a similar incident on the Western Front, when captured French aircrew are invited to lunch at a German mess by the officer who has shot them down. No. 14 Squadron's experience shows that this sort of thing really took place. For the 'Great War' was another world, as my father never tired of telling me. In his own words, in his own preferred language, *'autre temps, autre moeurs'* – different times, different behaviour.

Notes

1. T. E. Lawrence, *Seven Pillars of Wisdom*, p. 29.
2. This photograph is reproduced in *The Gnome*, May 1917, p. 1.
3. The Ottoman Air Force on the Sinai Front consisted of no more than a dozen pilots and observers in a single 'squadron' – in reality a flight – that in 1917 was based at El Kutrani.
4. Personal information from WELS (William Eric Louis Seward) to the author.
5. *The Gnome*, May 1917, p. 2. See also F. M. Cutlack, 'The Australian Flying Corps in the western and eastern theatres of war, 1914–1918', in *Official History of Australia in the War of 1914–1918*, p. 58.

CHAPTER 1

ROYAL FLYING CORPS OR AÉRONAUTIQUE MILITAIRE?

For all we have and are,
For all our children's fate,
Stand up and take the war,
The Hun is at the gate!

Rudyard Kipling, 'For All We Have and Are'

An only child, William Eric Louis Seward was born in 1891 at Toorak, Melbourne, where his father, William Arthur Seward, was a partner in Adet Seward et Cie, the first Bordeaux wine merchants to ship claret to Australia on a large scale. They were also the biggest exporters of Sauternes to Imperial Russia and cognac to Meiji Japan (from their own distillery at Cognac). Originally fanatical Puritans from the West Country, the Sewards had settled in County Cork during the seventeenth century, three of them serving in Cromwell's Army of Ireland – one as a cornet of horse. Later, they were mostly small landowners, merchants or lawyers. Their only really interesting member was the Dublin lawyer and antiquarian, William Wenman Seward, who in 1795 published *Topographica Hibernica*. When my father's branch left Ireland they converted to Catholicism.

A wild young Irishman, William Arthur Seward had liked living dangerously, trading for copra and sandalwood in the Trobriand Islands and New Caledonia (besides building a fine, pioneer collection of Oceanic art). In 1878 he and his not so adventurous brother Harry, who was reading for the Bar in London, more or less inherited the firm at Bordeaux from a French brother-in-law, and made their fortunes. However, in 1896 William died aged only 42, just after losing most of his Antipodean money during the great Melbourne slump – among other involvements he had been a director of five banks in Australia.

Taken back to Europe by his mother, born a Miss Eva Thunder, Eric spent his early years in France or in a farmhouse on what was left of his maternal grandfather's little estate at Ballycanew in County Wexford, where he was

Pierre de Beausire-Seyssel of the Aéronautique Militaire, the cousin who began WELS's interest in flying, about to take off from the aerodrome at Toussous-le-Noble in a Maurice Farman Longhorn, during the autumn of 1913. He spent 1915–18 as a prisoner of war and afterwards, unable to adapt to civilian life, threw himself out of a window in the Champs Elysées. (Author's collection)

largely brought up by his mother's parents. His grandfather, Andrew Thunder, had met his wife, the daughter of an Irish MP, in Paris where they were married at the British Embassy in 1862. They then lived for many years in Australia but, after Andrew had squandered a considerable fortune in a fruitless search for gold, came home to Ireland. The old couple always spoke French to each other. Mrs Thunder had passed an enchanted girlhood in Second Empire Paris where she had been presented to Empress Eugénie, while her brother and sisters had made French marriages. She gave her grandson a lasting regret that he had not been born a Frenchman, especially when they went to Paris. Hers was a very old-fashioned France, and she regarded the French Revolution as the worst catastrophe in history.

In France Eric was more or less adopted by relations and taken under the wing of his grandmother's sister, Christine de Sommyèvre, staying with her at her apartment just off the Champs Elysées, her château in Normandy or the Hôtel de Paris at Monte Carlo – of which she was a substantial shareholder. Her affection for him was due to the recent death of a son, killed in an accident at the Fontainebleau cavalry school. She took little Eric to the Révue de

Longchamps to see the red-trousered French Army march past – including cousins in glittering uniforms. She also brought him in a fast carriage to meets of the staghounds in the Norman forest at which members of the hunt wore swords, ladies gold-laced tricornes and officers full dress. They set off amid fanfares from a score of hunting horns, between rows of footmen bearing halberds, while in the evening the stag's body was fed to the hounds with great ceremony in the château courtyard, by the light of flaming torches and to the music of further braying fanfares. All this gave the boy a love of France and French tradition that endured for the rest of his life.

'La Tante Christine' was a royalist of the sort called a 'Blanc d'Espagne'. From her, he learned that the real French national anthem was not the 'Marseillaise' but 'Vive Henri Quatre', that on the infamous 14 July (Bastille Day) one must stay away from Paris, closing not only the gates but the shutters of one's château, that on 21 January (the day of Louis XVI's murder) men should wear black ties. He met the aged 'Tante Henriette' de Fréville, who remembered the court of the last king of France, Charles X. These Legitimist cousins in Paris were his mother's kindred, known as the 'French relations'.

In contrast, Seward cousins were known as the 'Bordeaux relations', though by now they spoke English with a French accent and were acquiring French wives or husbands. In their own way some of them were no less committed royalists than the Paris lot. Wearing hunt uniform and a hunting sword, Cousin Bertie Seward's father-in-law – Alphonse, Marquis d'Ayguesvyves – would ride performing cows to raise money for Action Française, which he identified with the cause of the Orleanist Pretender.

Today, Eric Seward's Ireland seems no less remote than his royalist France, the poverty-stricken if romantic land of Somerville and Ross, whom he remembered meeting. A man of majestic appearance, his grandfather was renowned for his kindness and the boy saw farmers kneel down to kiss his hand when he stopped his agent from raising their rents – everybody knew that he had difficulty in paying his own bills. Life here was very different from the luxury Eric was used to in France, but he learned how to ride and jump steep banks, how to cast a fly on the River Owenavarra. One memory was of visiting the seaside at Youghal and seeing the band of the local temperance society return from its annual outing to Cork – every man blind drunk save for the curate accompanying them, who ran round in tears, pulling bottles of stout or whiskey out of their pockets and smashing them on the station platform.

This is the type of plane in which WELS learned to fly during the autumn of 1915, an open-fuselage 1912 model Caudron, one of the standard training aircraft of the day. A 'tractor' (with the propeller in front), it had 'warping wings' and was powered by a 25 hp inverted 'Y' three-cylinder Anzani engine. (Philip Jarrett)

Yet Eric knew haunting stories of pre-famine Ireland, learned from old Andrew Thunder, who took the place of his father and enjoyed reminiscing with the boy. He told him of Jacobite forebears who served in the Irish Brigade fighting for France against Hanoverian England, of having met the last man condemned to be hanged, drawn and quartered (Smith O'Brien), of where to find gold in the Wicklow Hills 'but so little as not to be worth the mining', of how during the hot summer of 1839 the lake in front of a relative's house in County Meath had dried up, revealing a drowned crannog or Celtic water fortress. He also told him about his great-grandfather, Richard FitzGerald, MP for Tipperary, who had died in 1847 before Andrew married – one of the only two members of parliament to die of the 'Famine Fever'.

Throughout his life Eric Seward was never quite sure of his nationality or where he belonged. Even if he had comparatively little French blood – although very proud of his descent from a quaintly named Chevalier de l'Ecusson

Verdier – he was fanatically Francophile and is best described as a Franco-Irishman who sometimes tried to be British, if not always successfully. In his heart of hearts, he put more faith in Eternal France than in Holy Ireland or the British Empire, and was most at ease among Frenchmen despite speaking their language with a slight accent.

He had a difficult start. Dyslexic, he could not read properly until he was 13, so that he was unable to go as planned to Beaumont, the Jesuit school where his Seward cousins went; luckily he was sent to a tutor who specialized in such cases and who, besides giving him a sound education, instilled an abiding love of the classics. At the same time, he had inherited a need for violent exercise from his athletic mother, a superb horsewoman who in her youth had been known to ride 40 miles to a ball and then dance all night. Together, this induced a frustration that found vent in furious energy, mental and physical, and in a determination to excel – intensified by a healthy dash of insanity from his maternal forebears. When only 16, he was selected to swim for Britain in the Olympic Games of 1908, in the 100-metre backstroke race. Although beaten, he would later, while training, break the world record for the distance.

Articled to a City firm of accountants in 1911, but ultimately hoping to become a wine merchant in the family business at Bordeaux, he quickly found that he hated accountancy. Nor did he enjoy living in London. He tried to escape by joining the new Territorials (which he persisted in calling 'The Militia'), and learned how to ride with the Royal Horse Artillery – bareback, facing the horse's tail. He nearly died in 1912, however, after smashing his car (a chain-drive 'Lightning' Benz). Complications set in that were only healed by cutting two huge incisions in his back to drain his lungs. For a time his physique collapsed, although he retained gorilla-like arms and shoulders. It was the end of his career as an Olympic swimmer.

At the suggestion of his uncle, who had business interests there, he visited China and Japan. In China he smoked opium in the Shanghai Millionaires Club, which he found a good cure for a hangover, while at Canton he walked through the Street of Lepers for a bet; he did not care too much, however, for seeing criminals in bamboo cages and public beheadings around almost every corner. Crossing the Yangtze on a paddle steamer he noticed that men were hitching lifts by jumping from paddle to paddle. When one of them fell off, he tried to dive in and save him but was held back by the other passengers – while the man drowned he was told that, had he saved him, under Chinese law he would have been obliged to pay for his upkeep for the rest of his life.

A relative of his grandmother, Sir Conyngham Greene, was ambassador to Japan, and he enjoyed it far more there. In Kyoto an encounter with Prince Tokugawa, grandson of the last Shogun, resulted in some interesting introductions. He met fascinating old gentlemen with exquisite manners, who told him of samurai battles in which it was normal to see a head, shoulder and arm lopped off by a single blow from a sword. They found experts who taught him a lethal form of ju-jitsu.

As a young man, he was a mixture of shyness and berserk aggression. 'Where is that bloody fool? Oh, there you are,' must have been a fairly frequent form of address, judging from later life. Very good with his fists, he enjoyed challenging cab drivers to come down from their perch and fight for a sovereign if they were not satisfied with a tip. 'You can't do that sort of thing nowadays,' he would sigh nostalgically in later years. His nose had been broken long before he took to the air.

A fine shot, especially with a pistol, his favourite weapon was a .45-calibre Colt automatic because of its 'stopping power': he explained to me that it had been designed to fire a bullet that would knock a man off his feet if it failed to kill him. He was a competent swordsman with the épée and the sabre, and much admired his cousin Bertie Seward (who had fenced for Cambridge) for having fought a nearly fatal duel with the sword at Bordeaux. Among his other skills were throwing knives and boomerangs, including the difficult, bird-hunting sort. He also knew how to fight with a knife – 'coat over one's left arm, blade pointed at the brute's mouth, like an épée' – while he was the only man I ever met who could use a sling with any accuracy, taught by his grandfather.

The man who began his interest in flying was a cousin, Pierre, Vicomte de Beausire-Seyssel, the son of a member of Napoleon III's bodyguard. Having failed to enter the Military Academy at St Cyr, Pierre joined the Army and served in the ranks. When he joined the Aéronautique Militaire (forerunner of the Armée de l'Air) in 1912, his mother, who was Eric Seward's great-aunt and godmother, deluged the family with photographs of her aviator son in his box kite of an aeroplane. Despite being taken prisoner at the beginning of 1915 after a forced landing, and held in captivity for the rest of the war, Pierre remained an inspiration to his cousins.[1]

Many forget that for a few days during the autumn of 1914 it really did look as if the Germans were going to march into Paris. The French government fled to Bordeaux, and the British embassy went with it. The family did their best for the war effort, Bertie Seward installing half the embassy in his house.

(Afterwards, the Foreign Secretary, Sir Edward Grey, gave him a massive eighteenth-century silver standing salt as a token of gratitude.) Tante Christine de Sommyèvre lent her huge black and yellow Hispano-Suiza to ferry troops to the Battle of the Marne – three weeks later she was incensed to see the Minister of Defence's mistress being driven in it down the Champs Elysées.

In England pressure on young men to join up (conscription did not come until 1916) was unrelenting. Patriotism and enthusiasm for the cause of the 'Entente Powers' rose to a feverish intensity. Given half a chance, every band would strike up not only 'God Save the King', but the 'Marseillaise', 'God Preserve the Tsar', the 'Brabançon' and the Serbian national anthem. Young women with blazing eyes stuck white feathers into the buttonhole of any young man whom they suspected of being a 'trench-dodger', but there was no need for them to encourage my father. He loathed his profession and longed to join the Army. However, when he tried to enlist the doctors saw the scars on his back and declared him unfit for service with the armed forces.

Since Britain had no use for him, he decided that he would to learn to fly privately and join the Aéronautique Militaire. In 1914 twelve of his innumerable French kindred were officers in France's Army, as regulars or on the reserve, while, in addition to Pierre, two of them – Gaston d'Ayguesvyves and Raymond FitzGerald – were serving with the Aéronautique. Accordingly, he went to Hall's Flying School at Hendon where he was given lessons costing £75 in a Caudron (a 'tractor', with its propeller in front, as opposed to a 'pusher' with the propeller behind), in which he made his first solo flights. All you needed to qualify for a flying licence was to be able to take off, circle several times round a tall mast at the end of the aerodrome and land safely.[2]

Then an Irish cousin, Sir Michael O'Loghlen, Lieutenant for County Clare, intervened to ask Lord Hugh Cecil, a junior minister in charge of aviation, to let Seward join the RFC, on condition he 'served in a hot climate'. In November 1915 the War Office informed O'Loghlen that Seward was on the list to go to an Army Flying School. Equipped with a note from Cecil, he was summoned before a board.

The young man who presented himself at Room 26S of the War Office was 5 feet 8 inches tall, stocky, barrel-chested, red-headed and ugly-faced – even if he seems almost handsome in one or two photographs – with pale green eyes and a jutting chin. He had recovered from his motor accident and looked like the bruiser he was. The questions intrigued him. 'Do you hunt? Do you ride in point-to-points? Can you drive a four-in-hand or a pony and trap?'

All these questions were relevant in 1915, when a pilot needed a sensitive touch to master the instability of the period's primitive aircraft, by constantly adjusting his plane's balance with the lightest of touches on the joystick – it was not unlike riding a rather tricky horse.

Gazetted a second lieutenant in April 1916, he was sent to Oxford and billeted at Christ Church where, every day for three weeks, he was drilled for hours on end by NCOs from the Brigade of Guards, since the RFC used Guards' drill. Then he went to the flying school at Montrose in eastern Scotland, his CO being Euan Rabagliati, who had joined the RFC when it was founded in 1913. Even here, training meant little more than flying over to St Andrews, landing on the beach and strolling up into the elegant little city for afternoon tea. He was amused by the contrast between Montrose on Saturday nights, with the streets full of what appeared to be Harry Lauder's kinsmen waving whisky bottles, and Montrose on the sabbath – 'black crows crawling along to the kirk in hard hats, clutching bibles, and everybody looking as if they all had the most ghastly hangovers'.

In July 1916 Seward was given a passing-out certificate from the Central Flying School at Upavon on Salisbury Plain, and then orders to join No. 14 Squadron in Palestine. He prepared to go to the front in his usual, perfectionist way. His uniforms came from Jones, Chalk & Dawson in Sackville Street (including a 'British Warm' that cost 13 guineas), his field boots from Buhl (now merged with Lobb) and most of his other leather gear from Asprey. However, his flying helmet – a light leather cap, of which I still have the replacement, bought in 1917 – was purchased from André at 163 Piccadilly. He also acquired an American Navy Colt .45 automatic pistol, for which he was going to find a possible use that can never have been imagined in his wildest nightmares. At the beginning of August he embarked on a troop ship bound for Alexandria, a voyage that took about ten days, which he spent learning Arabic.

Notes

1. In 1909 the French Army began sending officers and NCOs to learn how to fly. The Aéronautique Militaire was formed in 1910, acquiring five squadrons of six aircraft by 1912. It remained part of the Army until 1936 when it became the Armée de l'Air.
2. On the back of a photograph taken at Hendon in September 1916 Seward wrote: '25 h.p. Caudron aeroplane (1912 model). Note: warped wings and Anzani three cylinder inverted "Y" type engine with ancillary exhaust ports.'

CHAPTER 2

THE BATTLE FOR THE
SUEZ CANAL, 1915–16

**'… that great and terrible wilderness, wherein
were fiery serpents, and scorpions, and drought,
where there was no water.'**

Deuteronomy, viii, 15

In 1915 the troops of the Entente occasionally left their trenches on the Western Front to fight the Germans at hideous cost for some small scrap of ground. In Eastern Europe Austria-Hungary and Germany waged a less static war against Russia and Serbia, with equally dreadful casualties. Italy joined the Entente, establishing a new front, while Bulgaria joined the Central Powers and created yet another. The Allied attempt to seize the Dardanelles at Gallipoli was heading for a humiliating failure. Everywhere the struggle became siege warfare on a massive scale, with neither side making progress.

During the first half of 1916 France and Germany inflicted terrible losses on each other at Verdun while from July Britain and Germany suffered appalling casualties on the Somme. Romania declared war on the Central Powers in August, but by the end of the year the Germans had occupied three-quarters of its territory, including Bucharest.

From the start the leaders of the Central Powers had seen the Suez Canal (running from the Mediterranean to the Red Sea through the Sinai Desert) as the British Empire's jugular vein, since it was Britain's route to India, along which passed not only Indian but Australian, New Zealand and South African troops. So important was the Canal for merchant shipping that during the war vessels were moored 15 or 20 miles up it. Even if they could not capture the Canal, a small Turkish army could at least tie down large quantities of troops and munitions needed elsewhere by the Allies. However, the enemy would have to attack across the Sinai.

The heart of the Sinai was a triangular waste of sand, crossed by camel routes, which met at El Arish near the Mediterranean Sea where the Turks

General Sir Archibald Murray, the former CIGS, who fancied himself as a commander in the field and was C-in-C Egyptian Expeditionary Force 1916–17. If a brilliant administrator, whose organisation paved the way for General Allenby's victories, he was both vain and neurotic. Before a meeting, T. E. Lawrence – the mildest-mannered of men – was asked by Murray's chief-of-staff 'not to frighten him'. (London Library)

established their advance headquarters. F. M. Cutlack described it as follows: 'It is mostly inhospitable desert, made the more hideous by great sand-hills heaped up by scorching winds – a vast waste of land whose dangers and loneliness are to the unsophisticated European as terrible as any sea. The tracks which reach out over it are routes that must often be followed rather by compass or stars than by landmarks.'[1] Along the coast a series of 'hods' – small oases amid palm trees – possessed surface wells which held a very limited supply of brackish water. This lack of water ruled out a British advance into enemy territory.

No troops were better suited to desert warfare than the Turkish infantry. While T. E. Lawrence dismissively called the *'askers'* an army of serfs, John Buchan (in his novel *Greenmantle*) thought they were 'as fanatical as the hordes of the Mahdi'.[2] Able to campaign for months on a few biscuits and a handful of dates, covering ground almost as fast as cavalry, they seemed to need much less water than their opponents. They had the good fortune to be commanded by a succession of gifted officers on loan from the German Army – Friedrich Freiherr Kress von Kressenstein, Erich von Falkenhayn and Otto Liman von Sanders – every one of whom led from the front.

The first of these commanders was a tall, skeletally thin, Bavarian gunner with a fleshless face adorned by pince-nez and a perpetual cigarette, in no way

The Savoy Hotel, Cairo, the best and most comfortable in the city, where the nervous General Murray installed his GHQ and a large staff. During his rare visits to the front, he insisted that three planes must fly above his armoured train at all times. WELS always referred to him as 'that damned old woman', a widely shared opinion. (Author's collection).

inhibited by lack of troops and weaponry. His attack on the Canal in February 1915, intended to bring about a pro-Turkish Egyptian revolt, was a failure, but no reverse ever dismayed him. Despite being heavily outnumbered, his 'Desert Force' continued to menace the border.

In contrast to Kress von Kressenstein, General Sir Archibald Murray, a former CIGS, who had taken over as Commander-in-Chief, Egyptian Expeditionary Force (EEF) at the beginning of 1916, was essentially a desk soldier. In his late fifties, a veteran of the Zululand campaigns, white-haired and with a lined, peevish countenance, he looked older than he was. Lawrence described him as 'all brains and claws, nervous, elastic, changeable'.[3] On one occasion Murray's Chief of Staff told Lawrence, 'Now you're not to frighten him: don't forget what I say!'[4] No doubt he was a gifted organiser who laid the foundations for his successor's triumph – camps, food stores and reservoirs, trailways, signal stations and ammunition depots. But he was no good at winning battles.

His GHQ was originally at Ismailia, the port at the mouth of the Canal that supplied fresh water and was the centre of his new rail network. Here, he sat down to plod on with his preparations. As Lawrence put it, 'Sir Archibald's army, probably the most cumbersome in the world, had to be laboriously pushed forward on its belly.'[5] But the Allies' evacuation of Gallipoli at the end of 1915 intensified the Turkish threat to the Canal, and even Murray was stung by Lord Kitchener's sneer that troops were supposed to defend the Canal and not the Canal the troops. Ponderously, he began to set in motion what he intended to be a methodical advance across the northern Sinai.

Early in autumn 1916 Murray moved his GHQ from Ismailia to the Savoy Hotel at Cairo in the Sharia Kasr-el-Nil, the city's most expensive hotel. (Crowned by a domed turret, it looked a bit like Harrods in London.) His staff grew to a size that many observers thought ludicrously inflated. Whenever he went to the front on a tour of inspection, which did not happen too often, he travelled in an armoured train, insisting that three aircraft fly overhead, just in case the enemy – no doubt well informed of his movements by Egyptian spies – should send planes to 'strafe' him. This infuriated the RFC who, in Seward's words, regarded their Commander-in-Chief at the Savoy Hotel as 'a damned old woman'.

There had been a more or less token RFC presence in Egypt since 1915, half a dozen Maurice Farmans and Henri Farmans, clumsy pushers, supported by French seaplanes from ships just off the coast. They were replaced in February 1916 by No. 14 Squadron of the RFC's 5th Wing. (A squadron was three flights of four machines.) It consisted of BE2Cs with a few Bristol Scouts, operating from a headquarters aerodrome at Ismailia and three auxiliary aerodromes on the Canal. Their main activity at this stage was reconnaissance and photography by BE2Cs, a plane whose range was 100 miles at most – and this only made possible by loading one of its cockpits with several cans of fuel.

The other half of the wing was No. 1 Squadron of the Australian Flying Corps, many of its personnel being former cavalrymen from the legendary Australian Light Horse, such as a certain Lieutenant Ross Smith. They were determined to do better than the Poms* and there was keen rivalry between the two squadrons, the British making jokes about the plumed headgear of Anzac cavalrymen as a sly dig at their neighbours. ('I think that hat would

---

* My father said that the word 'Pom' had emerged among the Australian Light Horse during the Boer War – accustomed to their own light saddles, they jeered that British troopers could only stay on their mounts by clinging to the high pommels of the heavy, regulation British cavalry saddles.

very well suit even a woman, don't you think so?' teased 'Major A. D. Fuze' in *The Gnome.*)[6] But nobody ever laughed about the fighting qualities of the Australians. Confusingly, until the creation of the Royal Air Force in 1918, No. 1 Squadron was known as 'No. 67 Squadron, RFC', although throughout this book it is always referred to as No. 1. Arriving in Egypt in the summer of 1916 with no machines and no trained pilots, within just a few weeks it was making a valuable contribution.

Meanwhile, the aircraft of No. 14 Squadron flew on a daily routine of reconnaissance and survey work. They also patrolled the three camel routes across the Sinai Desert over an area that extended 60 miles in front of the British lines, watching for any sign of an enemy advance. In addition, they made weekly bombing raids on Turkish strongpoints – notably on Bir el Hassana, Maghara and Rodh Salem. The object of these raids was to eliminate or, at the very least, to diminish the enemy's water supply.

Lieutenant Hill was particularly successful at Hassana, dropping a 20-lb bomb as a sighting shot within a few yards of the water tank, then following it up with another that exploded in the middle of the tank and destroyed the pumping machinery. After photographing the damage, Hill flew back to his aerodrome at Qantara. (The war diary thought it worthy of note that he covered a distance of 180 miles.) Next time, Hill was not so lucky, failing to return from a reconnaissance over Bir el Mazar and the Bardawi Lagoon. The aircraft that went to look for him could find no trace of pilot and machine. Eventually, secret agents discovered what had happened. Forced by engine trouble to land on the coast, for three hours he had used his machine-gun to hold off the Turkish patrols sent to capture him, until his ammunition ran out and he was taken prisoner.

The RFC's planes were backed up by the East Indies and Egypt Seaplane Squadron of the Royal Navy, which carried machines that until recently had been supporting the forces in Gallipoli and were flown by members of the Royal Naval Air Service. Led from May by the bearded Commander C. R. Samson, they too carried out reconnaissance and bombing missions. The 'Corps', including my father, disliked the RNAS, whom they regarded as pretentious and on the whole ineffectual, irreverently referring to the garrulous, boastful Samson as 'Flying Christ'. Even so, they were forced to cooperate closely since life was becoming much harder for both services.

In March two of the seaplanes had spotted half a dozen new aircraft hangars at Beersheba near the enemy headquarters and at El Arish on the

A two-seater Rumpler, the enemy equivalent of the BE2C, but superior in every way. (Unlike London, Berlin made a point of sending only the latest machines to the Middle East, which gave German pilots a technical advantage that lasted until the arrival of the Bristol Fighter late in 1917.) Although a reconnaissance plane, when the Rumpler arrived in the Sinai it turned out to be faster than most British 'scouts' and better armed. There were several models. This is the most formidable, a CIV. (Philip Jarrett)

coast. These hangars announced the arrival in Palestine of what in October 1916 would become known as the 'Luftstreitkräfte' (the German Imperial Air Service), in the form of Fliegerabteilung 300. Commanded by Hauptmann von Heemskerck, the pilots of this squadron seem to have been a very decent lot, as well as remarkably good pilots. The war diary and photographs in *The Gnome* show that among them were one or two Austro-Hungarian officers from the Kaiserliche und Königliche Luftfahrtruppen (Imperial and Royal Air Troops), who were probably regulars with a knowledge of Turkish picked up during garrison duty in the Balkans. Like the British and Australians, they were all convinced that their side was going to win the war.

Their machines included fourteen Rumpler C1 reconnaissance planes, two-seater biplanes that outpaced most of the British aircraft in the Sinai and climbed much faster. Since they could fly higher, they were often able to do their work unmolested. They also possessed several single-seater Pfalz EII scouts, which were armed with twin Spandau machine guns firing through

The DH1, a 'pusher' (with the propeller at the back), was so under-powered that none of these aircraft were sent to the Western Front and only a few to the Sinai. The last surviving specimen in Palestine, this one was shot down during a bombing raid on Tel el Sheria in March 1917. (Author's collection)

the propeller arc, and could dive at unusually high speed. This was the start of a depressing technical superiority of enemy machines over British ones on the Sinai front. 'It was not the German policy to relegate obsolete aeroplanes to subsidiary theatres of war', drily observe the authors of *The War in the Air.*[7] The Pfalz scouts were soon joined by Fokker monoplanes – the *Eindecker*, that scourge of the Western Front. Luckily for the British, the Germans in Palestine had comparatively few machines and were to remain outnumbered until October 1917.

Unlike the Western Front there were few dogfights at this stage of the campaign. Most hostile activity was confined to bombing, the British raiding El Arish and Beersheba while the Germans attacked Port Said. The RFC's missile was a 20-lb Spencer bomb, aimed by hand over the side of the cockpit, and the German version was about the same size. The British also dropped leaflets in Turkish and Arabic encouraging the enemy's troops to desert, although Turkish officers shot any soldier found reading them.

On 13 June 1916, on a probing skirmish on El Arish as a preliminary to a full-scale raid, No. 14 Squadron ran into one of the much feared Fokker monoplanes. But instead of a BE2C, the *Eindecker* attacked a DH1A pusher, which had no propeller in front to prevent its Lewis gun from firing forward. 'Our machine', says the diary, 'manoeuvred [so] as to keep above and behind

Right: Reconnaissance was the RFC's main job in the Sinai and in Palestine, as in France, searching for enemy troop movements and artillery batteries. Here is Captain T. C. Macaulay, the Intelligence Officer of 5th Wing, with whom pilots and observers of No. 14 Squadron worked closely. From The Gnome, *November 1916.* (Author's collection)

Colonel (later General) Friedrich, Freiherr Kress von Kressenstein, the Bavarian artilleryman who commanded the enemy so skilfully during the early stages of the Sinai campaign. Flying back from patrol in March 1917, WELS spotted Kress and his staff on their horses in the desert, but his Lewis gun jammed – he told me how much he had regretted not being able to kill them. (London Library)

the Fokker with the nose of the machine firing towards him, so that he could be ranged by our fire. This combat, which took place at 7,000 feet and for part of the engagement at a distance between the machines of fifty to seventy feet, was finally terminated by the German ... using his superior diving speed to escape.' The diarist adds proudly, 'Our one "Pusher" De Havilland two-seater fighter was always a terror to the enemy.'[8]

Whatever the diarist may say, the DH1 was far from Fokker-proof and the crew were lucky to survive. Underpowered, with a top speed of 80 mph, it was alarmingly vulnerable to attack from behind, but fortunately the *Eindecker* pilot – probably unaccustomed to his new plane – did not use the tactic of diving out of the sun that proved so effective on the Western Front. London had such a poor opinion of DH1s that none were sent to France and only a very few to the Middle East. Eventually, this sole surviving example was shot down by enemy anti-aircraft fire in March 1917, during a bombing raid on the Turkish railhead at Tel el Sheria.

The RFC's main attack, a week later, caught the enemy off guard. A total of 11 BE2Cs from Qantara (some used as single-seaters to carry heavier bombs) flew 10 miles out to sea before flying inland at a height of 7,000 ft and passing over the enemy aerodrome at El Arish. Then they circled back, coming down to 600 ft to drop their bombs – 76, according to German sources. Lieutenant Tipton went even lower, blowing to pieces an enemy machine, together with the mechanics frantically trying to get it into the air. In addition, two other enemy aircraft were destroyed, including a Pfalz and a Rumpler that had just taken off and already reached 100 ft. Also, six out of ten hangars were set on fire, two or three being burned to the ground, while seven ground crew were killed or badly injured. One of the British planes, descending to 200 ft, wound up this unusually successful attack with machine-gun fire.

The raiders did not escape unscathed. Three BE2Cs – flown as single-seaters – were brought down by anti-aircraft fire. Tipton was taken prisoner, but managed to escape. Lieutenant Van Ryneveldt (later the first man to fly from Egypt to the Cape) was forced to land on the shore amid the sand dunes after a bullet hit his engine sump, and burned his machine. However, another plane came down to his rescue, cramming him into the forward cockpit with the observer. Overloaded, soft sand clogging its wheels, it had trouble taking off, but somehow returned safely to base.

Defiantly, Fliegerabteilung 300 responded on the same day. That evening three of its undamaged Rumplers flew over Port Said and dropped 43 bombs.

In the summer of 1916 wireless (Morse code) was first used by the RFC during an army operation to destroy the wells at Wadi Muksheib. On one of the three main routes across the Sinai to Ismailia, these were about 40 miles away, the object being to prevent the Turks attacking across the desert from this direction. Squadron wireless personnel were attached to the column, and reconnaissance aircraft patrolling in front of its advance made regular reports by wireless or by dropping messages – handwritten notes, jotted down in the air.

The RFC had by now been reorganized. 5th Wing's HQ was still at Ismailia, with the headquarters' flight and one-and-a-half flights of No. 14 Squadron. Another flight was at Qantara, while the remaining half-flight was at Port Said. Qantara used 80 camels to bring up its petrol, sand carts (sledges) hauling its spare parts and tents. In addition, under 5th Wing's command were one-and-a-half flights of No. 1 Squadron of the Australian Flying Corps, the other half-flight being at Kharga in the Western Desert.

The first full-scale battle in Palestine in which the RFC and the AFC took part was at Romani in the summer. Both played a vital role in the build-up, reporting the approach of enemy forces as early as 19 July. When the enemy pushed their line forward on the night of 27–28 July, preparing for the offensive, every available machine – 17 in all – bombed them, breaking up their formations and hampering their communication and supply lines.

The Turks finally attacked on 3 August. However, Kress von Kressenstein could only muster 18,000 combat troops, who were driven off next day after some very hard fighting at bayonet point among the sandhills where the defenders had dug in. By the night of 5 August, the enemy were in full retreat, losing 4,000 prisoners. Nevertheless, they fell back so fast to El Arish, 50 miles behind, that the pursuit was unable to catch them. But the Suez Canal would never again be under threat.

During the engagement, Captain Grant-Dalton, flying a Bristol Scout, was attacked by three Aviatiks. Although badly wounded in a most unequal combat, he managed to land safely behind the British lines at Romani.

On 11 August a BE2C of No. 14 Squadron was not so lucky. Brigadier-General Chaytor, commanding the Anzac Division, was reconnoitring Bir el Abd on horseback when he saw enemy anti-aircraft guns shooting at a British aircraft. He says:

> Suddenly the anti-aircraft fire was switched off and an enemy aeroplane swooped down on ours which was apparently badly damaged, but shortly steadied and came down about three-quarters of a mile south-east of my headquarters. Captain Rhodes, my aide-de-camp, went off to locate the plane to give first aid, and I to headquarters to send an ambulance. On finding the plane Captain Rhodes found that the pilot, 2nd Lieut. E. W. Edwards, who was very badly wounded – I think seven bullets had hit him, one of which broke his lower jaw on both sides, another his shoulder – had gone off to get help for the observer who was shot in the chest and could not move. The observer, 2nd Lieut. J. Brown, though in great pain, refused to have his wounds attended to until he had made his report, as he said they had some important information and he was afraid he would faint if his wound was touched. He very gallantly held himself together until he had dictated his report and verified it and then, his duty done, fainted and died two hours later.[9]

The information seems to have been that the Turkish rearguard was withdrawing from Bir el Abd. The war diary provides further details. After the BE2C was attacked by two Aviatiks the pilot became unconscious from his wounds, only recovering when the plane was within 500 ft of the ground. The diary adds that Brown had been on his way back to England to train as a pilot when he learned that the enemy were advancing and immediately telephoned for permission to return and take part in the battle.[10]

Several other men had been seriously wounded, one mortally, while the Germans lost only a single machine, which was driven down out of control by an RFC scout over Salmana.

Another British aircraft, a BE2C operating from Suez, nearly became a casualty during a reconnaissance after the battle, when its engine cut out while flying over a mountain range in the southern Sinai. The pilot, Lieutenant Kingsley, spotted a flat surface on a mountain at the eastern end of the range where he could land, but which was opposite a Turkish outpost. He landed, nonetheless. While he repaired the engine trouble – a faulty magneto – his observer kept the Turks at bay with the Lewis gun when they climbed up a ravine to try and capture them. As soon as Kingsley had fixed the magneto, he dived the plane off the side of the mountain until its engine picked up, returning safely to base.[11]

When Seward joined No. 14 Squadron on 17 August, shortly after the Battle of Romani, the Egyptian Expeditionary Force was grinding forward along the coast, across the Sinai Desert. Troops were concentrated at points commanding the main routes. While large-scale defensive works were under construction, lightly held front-line positions were taken up, cavalry and camel columns patrolling the area in front of the enemy. Since half a million gallons of water a day were needed for Murray's forces, filtering, pumping and storage machinery had to be built to bring it from the Nile, together with a metal pipeline and a railway. The pipeline and railway ran from Qantara which, from a small 'native village', became a huge military base, canal port and depot.

On 4 September Captain Muir of No. 1 Squadron (and formerly of the Australian Light Horse) dropped 12 bombs with devastating effects on the Turks at Bir el Mazar, destroying tents and silencing several anti-aircraft guns. The Australian airmen were certainly beginning to punch their weight. A few days later they cooperated with Anzac cavalry in an attack on Bir el Mazar that forced a Turkish withdrawal.

Fliegerabteilung 300 fought back. When six Royal Naval Air Service planes appeared over El Arish on 17 September at 5.24 in the morning, with the object of directing naval guns on to the aerodrome, they were speedily chased away by two Rumplers flown by Oberleutnant Gerhard Felmy and Leutnant von Bülow-

Map 1: Suez and the Sinai desert.

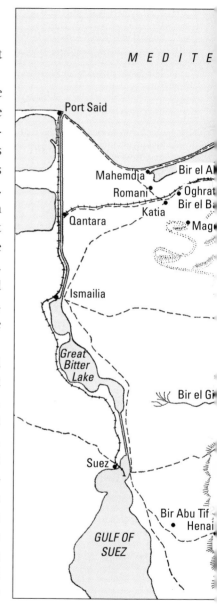

Bothkamp, and by a Pfalz scout flown by Leutnant von Hesler – all three still in their pyjamas.

Nevertheless, by mid-November 1916 the EEF was halfway to the Palestinian frontier. The objective was Kress von Kressenstein's head-quarters at El Arish, which has been described as the 'strategic pivot of the eastern Sinai'.[12] With its oases and sea port, in easy reach of enemy bases, it was not only the best possible position from which to defend Egypt and the Suez Canal, but also offered a springboard from which to invade Turkish Palestine. As the war diary comments, 'This pushing forward of our line necessitated the establishment of forward landing grounds, if contact with our advanced troops was to be effectively kept.'[13]

By the end of October No. 14 Squadron found itself operating from a forward aerodrome at Salmana. Within much closer range, on 11 November they bombed the German air base at Beersheba and the adjoining railway station, causing extensive damage. (I think this must have been when my father scored his first 'hit' – which he recalled as dropping a bomb between two locomotives and blowing them off the track.) Turkish troop camps at Magdhaba were also bombed. During the last week of November, the squadron's forward aerodrome was again moved – north, to Mustabig. They were accompanied by the Australians.

By 10 December the railway was within 20 miles of El Arish and, ten days later, the squadron's reconnaissance machines reported that the Turks were evacuating the town. Expecting a British attack from the sea, when none was planned, Kress von Kressenstein had decided to withdraw his army to Magdhaba and Rafa. General Sir Philip Chetwode's Desert Column marched

A N E A N

Hebron

Dead Sea

Gaza

Deir el Belah

Rafa

Irgeig

Weli Sheikh Nuran

Beersheba

Sheikh Zowaiid

El Arish

Khalasa

Imana

Bir el Mazar

r el Ganadil

Wadi

N D *D U N E S*

U N E S

Magdhaba

Abu Aweigila

El Auja

El Ruafa

el Arish

El Kossaima

TURCO-EGYPTIAN FRONTIER

Bir el Hassana

Bir el Themada

10 5 0   10   20   30

SCALE: MILES

Sudr

Nekhl

Wadi el Arish

Akaba

into El Arish on 21 December. Magdhaba fell the following day, but Rafa held
out stubbornly until 8 January 1917. Kress von Kressenstein had wanted to
pull back the troops defending Magdhaba, but since it was one of Turkey's last
footholds in the Sinai, Djemal Pasha, who was the overall commander in the
region, would not let them withdraw.

No. 14 Squadron and No. 1 Squadron distinguished themselves during what the staff quaintly called 'The Affair of Magdhaba' – 13 BE2Cs dropped 120 x 16-lb or 20-lb bombs on the beleaguered Turks, together with six 100-lb bombs. If ludicrously small by later standards, these 'hundred-pounders' were monsters for the period. On the day before, 21 December, No. 14 Squadron had attacked and seriously damaged a railway bridge just north of Beersheba.

One foggy morning at the end of the month the visibility suddenly improved and, about 20 miles south of El Arish, from his BE2C a pilot suddenly saw two Turkish battalions withdrawing. After he had flown back to report, 11 aircraft returned to strafe them with bombs and machine-gun fire. Suffering heavy casualties, the enemy force disintegrated, survivors fleeing into the desert.

Kress von Kressenstein regrouped the Turks, digging in on a knoll in front of Rafa. His work parties were bombed daily by British planes, which took photographs of the trenches, providing a map to direct artillery fire. On the night of 8/9 January 1917 in 'The Action of Rafah', the Australian Light Horse surrounded the position, then stormed it at bayonet point. No. 14 Squadron helped by bombing and directing artillery fire. The enemy aerodrome at Beersheba was under constant attack, while attempts were made to intercept any German machine that appeared in the sky.

These attempts were not always successful. Lieutenant Kingsley of No. 14 Squadron, apparently in a Martinsyde scout, flew up with suicidal bravery to engage two Fokker monoplanes and an Aviatik two-seater. Within minutes he had been wounded twice, while another bullet went through his petrol tank. Making for the coast before his fuel leaked away, he dropped his bombs on any Turkish encampments he flew over and then ditched his plane in the sea north of Rafa. Trying to reach the British lines, he was captured by a group of Bedouins, who stripped him naked. Luckily, he was rescued by a patrol of Australian cavalry.

Throughout the engagement British aircraft attacked the enemy from a low altitude, using bombs and machine guns. Turkish troops on the march were shot up and motor convoys destroyed. Infantry in the trenches and gun crews in the batteries were similarly strafed from a height of only 200 or 300 ft. The Turks became so fearful that their patrols and front-line troops were ordered to send up smoke signals as soon as they spotted a British aircraft. The enemy also enlisted the help of the Bedouin, but British planes machine-gunned any found signalling, which put an end to the practice.

After the fall of Rafa, 5th Wing's aeroplanes attacked Beersheba railway station and aerodrome incessantly, both by day and – when the moon was full – by night. Bombing parties generally consisted of three Martinsydes escorted by three Bristol Scouts. The Germans were forced to abandon the aerodrome, using it only as an occasional landing ground, and had to establish a new base 30 miles north, at Ramleh. This, too, was soon under constant attack. Later, the Luftstreitkräfte moved back for a time to Beersheba, but was again forced to evacuate.

The other main bombing target was Junction Station. Here the railway from Jaffa to Jerusalem joined the line running south to Beersheba, along which travelled all Turkish reinforcements and munitions. It was also the starting point of a new line that the enemy was building in order to supply the eastern section of the Gaza–Beersheba Front.

In the meantime, British Sappers had been laying the tracks for the EEF's own railway from Ismailia, which now extended as far as Rafa. The logistic infrastructure was in place. Even General Sir Archibald Murray was ready to advance into Turkish Palestine.

Notes

1. F. M. Cutlack, 'The Australian Flying Corps in the western and eastern theatres of war, 1914–1918', p. 53.
2. J. Buchan, *Greenmantle*, p. 6.
3. T. E. Lawrence, *Seven Pillars of Wisdom*, p. 329.
4. *Ibid.*, p. 114.
5. *Ibid.*, p. 203.
6. *The Gnome*, January 1917, p. 16.
7. W. Raleigh and H. A. Jones, *The War in the Air*, Vol. V, p. 179.
8. 'Operations Record Book, No. 14 (Bombing) Squadron', pp. 9–10.
9. Raleigh and Jones, *The War in the Air*, Vol. V, p. 195.
10. 'Operations Record Book', p. 56.
11. *Ibid.*, p. 17.
12. D. L. Bullock, *Allenby's War*, p. 31.
13. 'Operations Record Book', p. 18.

CHAPTER 3

PLANES AND PERSONNEL

**'He found himself in a desert land, in a place
of horror, and of vast wilderness.'**

Deuteronomy, xxxii, 10

When Seward landed at Alexandria in August 1916, he learned that he had been posted to Ismailia. According to the war diary, in those days this was:

> . . . a small French town, situated on Lake Timsah and flanking the Suez Canal, the headquarters of [the] Canal organisation, an oasis of shade and tropical luxuriance in striking contrast with the hard, glaring desert that surrounds it, designed and laid out with that happy symmetry in which the French excel, fated to be all that most of the Squadron were to see of civilisation for many a day. The aerodrome was on the north west side of the town, about a mile from it. It consisted of a number of wooden hangars surrounded by tents and a few huts.[1]

Every officer had his own surprisingly spacious tent. Its furniture consisted of a camp bed (with mosquito net), a folding table, a deckchair, an oil lamp, and a white enamel basin for ablutions. There was no wash jug, hot water being brought by a batman in the mornings.

Seward's duties were not what he expected. Like most people he was under the impression that the RFC's main job consisted of 'dogfights'. Liddell Hart writes of the 'Homeric combats of individual champions – whose mounting score of victims had been followed with the excitement that formerly awaited the return of a Red Indian scalping expedition or the news of a test match.'[2] But so far these duels were rare in the Middle East, where air fighting had not developed so quickly as in France because of the long distances between British and German aerodromes. Machines with such a short range could only engage each other for a few minutes – although this would change when the distances grew shorter. Instead, aircrew surveyed, mapped and photographed the Sinai, in readiness for the invasion of Palestine. At the same time, they

WELS shortly after his arrival at Ismailia aerodrome in September 1916 and finding the heat 'perfectly beastly'. This is not surprising as he is wearing a 'sola topi', in those days considered essential for protection against the sun, and under his shirt a bulky flannel 'cholera belt' that makes him look fatter than he really was; later he discarded both topi and cholera belt. (Author's collection)

WELS's photograph of No. 14 Squadron's wooden aircraft hangars at Ismailia, late 1917. (Author's collection)

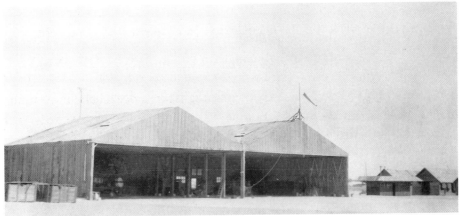

watched for troop movements or build-ups that indicated an enemy attack. They also helped to direct artillery fire, cooperating closely with the gunners on the ground.

Aerial photography entailed using a special Thornton-Picard camera of 20-inch focal length (in a square mahogany box fitted to the side of the pilot's cockpit) and glass plates. Leaning over the side, the pilot photographed the

WELS piloting a BE2C is being briefed by Captain Albrecht, the adjutant of No. 14 Squadron, before taking off from the aerodrome at Ismailia on a long reconnaissance flight over the Sinai Desert, October or November 1916. At that date the main danger, apart from the perennial hazards of engine failure and a forced landing without wireless or water, was attack by Fokker monoplanes. (Author's collection)

feature required by sighting it through a ball-and-crosswire 'finder', which was also at the side of the cockpit, and then pulling a cord for each exposure. It was not an easy business, especially in a strong wind, as he had to fly the plane with his left hand while changing the plates, which might easily be blown out of his grasp. But by autumn 1917 all southern Palestine had been surveyed in this way, providing 1:20,000 scale maps.

Despite its clumsy, four-bladed, mahogany propeller, the two-seater BE2C biplane used for this tedious job had some good points. The war diary says that, 'when treated with that affectionate care which good pilots and mechanics give – a care all the more needed in a sand blown country', its air-cooled RAF (Royal Aircraft Factory) engine was unusually reliable. Unlike most other planes at this stage of the war, it was inherently stable, which made it an ideal camera platform. 'If, in the later stages of the campaign it was superseded by types giving greater potency of climb and speed, and machines of [a] design more suited to the whirling manoeuvres of air-fighting replaced the old B.E., no one forgot its steady record in the prosaic gradgrind of desert reconnaissance.'[3]

The BE2C pictured on the previous page, about to take off. Because of its stability in the air, this type of machine (nicknamed 'Stability Jane') made an ideal camera platform for photographing enemy troop dispositions and fortifications – the RFC's main function at this stage of the war – but it was dangerously vulnerable to attack by hostile aircraft. (Author's collection)

Unfortunately, 'Stability Jane' was slow and clumsy, and although armed with a Lewis machine gun, more or less defenceless. Standing up in the forward cockpit, the observer who fired the gun over the head of the pilot behind him was so hemmed in by struts and wires that he could do little to fend off a determined enemy. Now that Fokkers had arrived, BE2Cs had to be escorted by scout fighters. By late 1916 these were Martinsyde 'Elephants', the top speed of which was only 87 mph. Unstable, sluggish in responding to controls, they were difficult to fly; in France so many had been shot down in dogfights with Fokkers that they were withdrawn from service.

Like the Bristol Scouts they were replacing, each Martinsyde was armed with a Lewis gun mounted on the centre section of the upper wing, firing outside the radius of the propeller blades. The Lewis gun – standard armament on all British planes at this date – was notoriously unreliable, prone to jam at crucial moments. Its ammunition drum (holding 47 rounds, afterwards increased to 98) was quickly exhausted. Nor were the drums easy to change in the air, especially during combat with an enemy aircraft, since it meant the pilot standing up and leaving the aircraft to fly itself for several vital moments.

His superiors quickly realized that Seward was a natural pilot. After a few patrols in a BE2C – which often meant no more than chauffeuring an observer – he was given one of the Squadron's few Bristol Scouts. Not to be confused with the Bristol Fighter that appeared later, this was a tiny, single-seater, not very fast but wonderfully manoeuvrable. Only 20 ft long, with a wingspan of just 24 ft 7 in, he liked to recall that 'it would easily have fitted into a small-sized drawing-room'. (The cockpit was so cramped that 'even an average man had to be eased in with a shoehorn', wrote Cecil Lewis in *Farewell to Wings*.) Yet my father told me he always felt safe in one of these little planes, even when being chased by a determined Hun flying a faster machine. Its top speed was 94 mph while it could climb to 6,500 ft in 10 minutes. Its ceiling was 15,500 ft, although it was seldom flown so high because of the cold.

However, he often found himself back in a BE2C since, like every other aircraft in the Sinai, the Bristol Scout was always breaking down and being grounded for repairs. Pilots had to take what was available, whether a single-seater or a two-seater. Because of casualties sometimes they acted as observers.

He became so fond of his Bristol that *The Gnome* published a poem about him (he was nicknamed 'Seaweed'):

> 'Seaweed' had a pet machine
> Which no one else might fly
> And everywhere that 'Seaweed' went
> He kept that Bristol nigh.
> He took her for a flight one day,
> Yes, right above the ground!
> He climbed her several hundred feet
> And flew her round and round;
> And all went well till came the time
> For him to wander home;
> He brought her humming down again
> Into the Aerodrome.
> Then what a sorry sight is seen,
> Upon her nose she's standing,
> The which may well explain the term
> 'A perfect Seaweed landing'.

A Bristol Scout, WELS's favourite aircraft, normally armed with a Lewis gun on the top plane. Although very small, comparatively slow and soon outdated, it was exceptionally manoeuvrable so that he always felt perfectly safe when attacked by faster, better-armed, German machines such as the Fokker monoplanes. He said that in any case it was always fun to fly. November or December 1916. (Author's collection)

He never could bear being laughed at, and wrote on the magazine cover, 'I did not crash as stated. I was supposed to be very good at landing. W. E. L. S.' Even so, he had a real gift for flying, becoming the squadron's unofficial test pilot. This not only meant putting newly arrived machines through their paces, but checking those that had been damaged and repaired before they went back into service – a hazardous job, in the end it was his undoing.[4]

On the ground, he must have seemed a bit of an oddity to his new brother officers, never having gone to a school or a university, and with his slightly French ways, if his manners and speech appeared English enough. He resembled many Frenchmen of those days in not making friends easily with people who were not relations. Oddest of all, he did not come from the Army. Although a mixed lot, at that date, with rare exceptions everybody else had been a soldier in the trenches, if not a regular. The May 1917 issue of *The Gnome* contained a doggerel poem by 'C. F.' that makes this point very well:

R.F.C.

(With apologies to Rudyard Kipling)

I used to be in the Scots Guards once –
Sussex, Lincolns and Rifles once –
Yorkshire, Derbys, and Civies once –
But now I am R.F.C. ...

We used to talk of horses once –
of bayonets, rifles and lances once –
But now there's the R.F.C. ...

I used to belong to an army once –
Dear little crawling army once –
Trudging thro' mud as I route-marched once,
But now I am R.F.C.

Despite being such an odd fish, from the start Seward's toughness – No. 14 Squadron could tell a bruiser when it saw one – and his dedication to flying earned him respect. In addition to being called 'Seaweed' by witty brother officers, he was also known as 'Old Glorious' by the men (due to his invariable response when asked how a patrol had gone – 'perfectly glorious'). Somehow, he managed to keep his terrifying temper under control – 'he'd knock you down for nothing', said a friend who knew him – although his idea of the right way to start an argument was to go in and kick the table over. He also softened his arrogant manner with strangers by adopting a permanent, slightly vulpine grin. Fortunately, he got on well with his superior officers.

The senior of these was Brigadier-General W. G. H. Salmond, who would end his career as Chief of the Air Staff. In 1916 he was 38 years old and as a Gunner he had fought Boers in South Africa and Boxers in China, before joining the RFC in 1913. Still only a captain when war broke out, he became an airborne Old Contemptible, and saw plenty of action on the Western Front before his posting to RFC Middle East Brigade. Ferret-faced but jolly, if occasionally waspish, Geoffrey Salmond was the man who, apart from a brief interval, directed flying not only in Egypt and Palestine, but also in Mesopotamia, East Africa and Salonika until the end of the war. 'He had

Left: *Brigadier-General Geoffrey Salmond, a future Chief of the Air Staff, who led the RFC and later the RAF in Palestine. From* The Gnome, *March 1917.* (Author's collection)

Left: *Lieutenant-Colonel A.E. ('Biffy') Borton, DSO, later an air vice-marshal, who became commander of 5th Wing in the spring of 1917. Originally in the Black Watch and then another pre-war RFC officer, he was the inventor of the term 'Archie' for anti-aircraft fire – inspired by George Roby's coarse music-hall song, 'Not tonight, Archibald!' Very popular, he worked closely with Salmond.* (London Library)

Right: *From right, WELS and Lieutenant-Colonel P. B. Joubert de la Ferté in relaxed mood at Ismailia. Joubert (later clean-shaven) became an air marshal. Late 1916.*
(Author's collection)

experience, vision, sane judgement and great charm of manner, a combination of qualities which enabled him to get things done with the minimum of fuss', wrote H. A. Jones in *The War in the Air*.[5] Keen that ground troops should understand what the RFC was all about, he started lectures for Army officers on its organization and raison d'être.[6]

Seward liked not only Salmond but the commander of 5th Wing, Lieutenant-Colonel P. B. Joubert de la Ferté (also a pre-war RFC officer) a swarthy man with a big black moustache which he later shaved off. His job resembled a squadron leader's in the future RAF, so there was plenty of contact between wing commander and pilots – a photograph shows Seward and Joubert sharing what appears to have been a very good joke. Joubert stayed on in the service after the war, ending his career as an air marshal.[7]

He liked even more another pre-war RFC officer, who took over from Joubert as the wing commander in spring 1917. This was the amiable Amyas Borton, full of jokes, a regular who had begun as a subaltern in the Black Watch. He had seen plenty of air fighting in France and at Gallipoli, where he had received a bullet through the jaw in a dogfight and been recommended for a Victoria Cross, although awarded only a DSO. He ended as an air vice-marshal.[8]

Captain Albrecht, the otter hunter, with his terrier – brought out from England – at Kilo 143, spring 1917. Teased because of his German name, but much liked by his brother officers, he was popularly known as 'The Count'. Albrecht was later 'killed in action'. (Author's collection)

Seward was also on good terms with his adjutant, Captain Vaudrey Adolph Albrecht, known in the squadron as the 'Count' because of his German name, although no one could have been more English. When at home in the summer, he delighted in otter hunting, that long-forgotten country sport, the 'cricket of hunting' in which even Sir Edward Elgar indulged, nowadays only remembered from Henry Williamson's *Tarka the Otter*. Albrecht used to speak with nostalgia of otter hunts in Devon along what was known as 'the gentleman's river', because it had a bridge every quarter of a mile with a pub in which hunt followers could quench their thirst. Sadly, he would not survive the war.

On the whole, Seward got on with his new comrades. Up to a point, he admired them, adopting their vocabulary and mannerisms, and outwardly becoming very much a British officer, concealing the Gallic aspects of his personality. Occasionally these emerged, however, including a startling habit of swearing in French, while to show sympathy with bereavement he would twist his face into a mask of sorrow that could have a devastating effect on English restraint.

Deeply reserved, he made few real friends, though. The exceptions were Harold Freeman, Stuart Reid and, to a lesser extent, J. E. Dixon-Spain.

Major H. R. Freeman, No. 14 Squadron's star pilot and WELS's closest friend in the Sinai, as he shared his interest in history. Later, having achieved his aim of being transferred to the Western Front, Freeman attacked six enemy planes single-handed and accounted for four before he was shot down in flames. (Author's collection)

Freeman, a former medical student, was No. 14 Squadron's star pilot, a handsome, slightly-built young man with a serious, sensitive face, who was obsessed with shooting down Huns. Judging from his letters, there was something oddly immature about him: when he commanded the Squadron his attitude resembled that of the captain of a public-school cricket team. But nobody could deny his bravery, of the sort he had shown in December 1916, when on reconnaissance with Lieutenant F. Minchin over Beersheba. Both in Martinsydes, they were intercepted by an Aviatik and two Fokker monoplanes. Minchin's machine was so badly damaged by machine-gun fire that he was forced to land in the desert behind enemy lines near Rafa, where he burned his plane and waited to be taken prisoner. However, Freeman landed, crammed him into the tiny cockpit of his own Martinsyde and then flew safely back to base, despite being chased by the Germans.

While Seward respected Freeman's skills as a pilot, what he liked was his conversation. The pair shared a deep love of history, and a passion for archaeology. They were thrilled to find themselves living in the land of the Bible.

A New Zealander born in 1883, William Stuart Reid was an artist by profession, who had studied in London and Munich, and at the Glasgow

'Fred' Minchin of No. 14 Squadron was always unlucky. On one occasion when his machine went down over enemy territory he was rescued by Freeman, who crammed him into the cockpit of his own single-seater. He disappeared in 1927 while trying to fly the Atlantic from England after being last seen off the Newfoundland coast. Note his odd flying gear, suitable for the heat at low altitudes – an RFC 'maternity jacket' and shorts. From The Gnome, *November 1916. (Author's collection)*

School of Art, specialising in studies of the female nude and race horses. Tough and adventurous, during the Boer War he had served in South Africa with a Yeomanry regiment, Tullibardine's Horse. A tall, lean man, always in riding breeches, sparing of speech and with a sardonic wit, his face wore a cheerful, slightly wicked expression, while he was good at laughing at himself. Somebody with an admiring eye for Egyptian girls – not entirely an artist's eye, one suspects – it also seems he was excellent company.[9]

The brainiest of the three was Captain (later Lieutenant-Colonel) J. E. Dixon-Spain, who had joined the Squadron in March 1916, after serving with the Hampshire Regiment, and remained with it until spring 1918. Already 36 when war broke out, the son of a Lincolnshire parson, he was a short, stocky, bald, somewhat undistinguished-looking figure with goggle eyes, an architect by profession, who had served as a volunteer in the Yeomanry during the Boer War, being awarded the unusual rank of 'honorary lieutenant'. Bursting with ideas, in August 1916 he started a 'Technical Training Class' in the ante-room of the mess where, together with experienced NCOs, he gave lectures on engine problems, rigging and gunnery, and even set an examination paper. (This was the origin of No. 3 School of Military Aeronautics at Heliopolis.) He was also the

*Another of WEL's few close friends,
Stuart Reid, off duty on the aerodrome
at Kilo 143. A New Zealander, during
the Boer War he had served with
Tullibardine's Horse in South Africa,
but in peacetime was a painter who
specialised in the female nude and race
horses – the former much appreciated by
WELS.* (Author's collection)

founder and moving spirit of *The Gnome*, which he edited while on active service with the squadron, revealing a good deal about himself in his editorials.

Dixon-Spain's flying log book has survived but, like all documents of its sort, is not particularly illuminating. Yet its constant references to engine failure, forced landings and broken undercarriages hint at the unremitting strain on pilots. There is one unmistakably grim entry – 'searching for Wilson' – who presumably was a brother officer lost in the wastes of the Sinai.[10]

Other members of the squadron included the swaggering, monocled Dempsey, once of the Foreign Legion's two short-lived squadrons of cavalry (and therefore able to speak French, 'of a sort'). There was also an ex-Foreign Legion doctor, who after dinner in the mess would pass round as a curiosity his tobacco pouch, made from the thigh of an African who had tried to knife him in Mauretania. Some members would stay in the service after the war, reaching high rank. Willock became an air marshal, Offerd an air commodore. The former, 'Wilber', a congenial soul, was famous for relying on the slipstream past his cockpit to cure hangovers.

While there were a fair number of sergeant pilots in squadrons on the Western Front, in the Sinai according to Seward, 'We had a few but they weren't

Three Australian friends photographed by WELS in September 1917. Written on the back is 'Scottie Glen, Mustard, Dingbat, of No. 1 Squadron, AFC.' Lieutenant A. E. Mustard frequently flew as the famous Ross Smith's observer in a Bristol Fighter. Largely recruited from the Australian Light Horse, the pilots of No. 1 Squadron were a particularly fine lot. (Author's collection)

much good.' At least one of the ground crew resented not being allowed to fly. This was Flight Sergeant C. R. King, who began the war in 1914 as a rigger at the Central Flying School, Upavon, and then served as an observer with the Squadron in France before moving with it to the Sinai Front. (His manuscript memoirs are at the Imperial War Museum.) His exclusion may not have been for social reasons, however, as he failed to obtain a commission in 1918, when many men were promoted from the ranks.

The Australians, No. 14 Squadron's closest neighbours and comrades as well as rivals, seem to have been a splendid bunch. As many had served with the Australian Light Horse, they showed all the dash and pugnacity of their old regiments. Seward got on well with them, which was scarcely surprising since he had relations in Australia. (The most interesting was an uncle, the Irish baronet Sir Michael O'Loghlen, MP for County Clare and during the 1880s Prime Minister for Victoria – the last man to sit simultaneously in the House of Commons and a 'colonial legislature' – whose son had helped Seward join the RFC.) Among new acquaintances in No. 1 Squadron were Captain Ross Smith, who in 1919 would become the first man to fly from England to Australia, and his tough little observer, the aptly named Lieutenant Mustard. They appear in my father's photographs, together with someone called 'Dingbat'.

Both British and Australian pilots were extremely proud of their wartime profession. In 1917, clearly with whole-hearted approval, *The Gnome* reprinted part of the obituary in *The Times* of Captain Lord Lucas, RFC – the model for Sandy Arbuthnot in Buchan's novel *Greenmantle* – who had been shot down at the end of the previous year.

> Everyone who knew him will be glad that if he had to die he died in the air. It is an assurance to them that he was happy to the last, pursuing and pursued up there, exulting in it all, even in the last moment when he had the supreme experience. No ill-will, I am sure, to whoever brought him down, but rather a wave of the hand from one airman to another. There is still that sort of chivalry on both sides in the sky. Having had a very good life in the years that he spent on the ground, they nevertheless seemed strange and stupid to him after his first flight. He came down a different man from the one who went up, and was different ever afterwards, as if he had made a journey into the springtime of the world and brought back a breath of it. This is what it is to be a true airman; you may see the same look in all their faces. It is not to be wondered at that so many of them fly away and never come back.[11]

Notes

1. 'Operations Record Book, No. 14 (Bombing) Squadron', p. 3.
2. Sir Basil Liddell Hart, *A History of the World War, 1914–1918*, p. 460.
3. 'Operations Record Book', p. 3.
4. *The Gnome*, August 1917, p. 7.
5. W. Raleigh and H. A. Jones, *The War in the Air*, Vol. V, p. 457.
6. See A. Baker, *From Biplane to Spitfire: The Life of Air Chief Marshal Sir Geoffrey Salmond*.
7. See P. B. Joubert de la Ferté, *The Third Service*, 1955.
8. See J. Slater (ed.), *My Warrior Sons: The Borton Family Diaries*.
9. See the *Australian Magazine*, November 1950.
10. J. E. Dixon-Spain, 'Flying Logbook, 23 June 1915 to 18 April 1918', Department of Documents, Imperial War Museum.
11. *The Gnome*, August 1917, quoting from J. M. Barrie's appreciation in *The Times* in December 1916.

CHAPTER 4

FLYING ABOVE THE SINAI DESERT

This is the song of the Plane –
The creaking, shrieking plane,
The throbbing, sobbing plane,
And the moaning, groaning wires: –
The engine – missing again!
One cylinder never fires!
Hey ho! for the Plane.'

Captain Gordon Alchin, RFC, 'A Song of the Plane'

In mid-January 1917 No. 14 Squadron and No. 1 Squadron moved to the former German aerodrome at Ujret el Zol in the desert. This was 5 miles west of El Arish, a tiny, picturesque, oasis town near the Mediterranean that was ringed by palm trees. An entire village of canvas and wood sprang up: hangars, stores, offices, workshops, barracks and mess tents, with a tent for each officer. Carried from the shore on camels or sand carts, during the initial stages petrol, oil, spare parts, ammunition, food and other supplies were brought in by sea from Egypt. The authorities named the new base 'Kilo 143'. It was to be Seward's home for the first months of 1917.

Canvas hangar at Kilo 143, early 1917. (Author's collection)

Camels bringing building materials to the new aerodrome at Kilo 143 near El Arish – they were even used to carry petrol and ammunition that had been landed on the coast. Note the BE2C in the background. February 1917. (Author's collection)

Other ranks playing the fool. The 'troops', as RFC officers called them, worked tirelessly to service aircraft. The heat often made it necessary for the dope proofing on the canvas-covered wings and fuselage to be stripped off and replaced overnight. Their lives were usually safe enough, however, as they did not fly. (Author's collection)

In the sky, the noise and smell of flying – and the danger – were much the same over the Sinai as they were over the Western Front. The loud, chattering purr of the engine, the howl of the wind as it rushed through the struts and brace wires that held together the plane's upper and lower wings – deafening in an open canvas cockpit – together with the reek of petrol or of burned castor oil, which lubricated the rotary Gnome engines that powered most British aircraft, or of the dope on a newly re-varnished cockpit. Often, the oil drenched both pilot and windscreen, blacking out everything before being wiped away in frantic haste. As in France, engines were always stopping without warning, struts and wires snapping, canvas ripping off wings and tail planes, undercarriages collapsing – and if a plane turned too sharply, its wings might break off.

But flying such primitive machines in the desert brought problems unknown in France. Between May and July the heat in the desert rose to 117°F in the shade, making operations very nearly impossible. In theory, aircraft could function up to a point as it was cooler in the clouds, but frequently their engines boiled over; in any case, 50 per cent of the petrol in the tank evaporated at such temperatures, severely decreasing a plane's range – short as it was. Another hazard was the scorching sandstorms; always unpredictable, these might suddenly blow up, rising as high as 2,000 ft. On the ground, stationary propellers (made of laminated mahogany) sometimes warped until they split apart, or rubber tyres would suddenly burst. The dope that varnished the canvas wings and fuselage cracked within a week under prolonged exposure to the sun, and had to be stripped off and replaced by sweating, overworked mechanics.

Even during milder months when the heat was not so ferocious, there were perils never dreamed of by the RFC in France. 'Engine failure meant a desert landing in a waterless, almost trackless region with ever shifting sands modifying the landscape; and a weary trek of days by compass bearing until the sight of canal or lakes gave the thirsty journeyer assurance of a safe return', records the war diary, a little too optimistically.[1] The author admits that the main requirement 'to master the flying difficulties of these strange and novel conditions' was a reliable engine, but he must have known very well that no such thing existed in 1916.

What the war diary does not spell out is that a forced landing in the parched, waterless Sinai could mean an agonising death from thirst. Planes were not yet equipped with a wireless on which they could call for help, and acute dehydration set in quickly under such ferocious heat. A painting by Stuart Reid in the Imperial War Museum, *The Ridley Tragedy* (originally called *The Great Sacrifice*) shows a catastrophe of this sort that took place not in the Sinai but in the Western Desert.

PITTERS AT POKER

Much of the evenings at Kilo 143 were spent playing poker – 'Pitters' was No. 14
Squadron's wireless expert, 'wireless' meaning Morse code. From The Gnome, *May 1917.*
(Author's collection)

On 15 June 1916, at the very hottest time of the year, two BE2Cs from
No. 17 Squadron lost their bearings here and were overtaken by nightfall. Next
morning, the engine of one plane would not start so the other flew off to get
help. When the pilot returned there was no sign of his comrades. Afterwards,
it was learned they had succeeded in making their engine start, but then had
to make two more forced landings, the second being final with the engine a
write-off. When a camel patrol found them on 20 June, the crew were both
dead. In his diary the observer, First Air Mechanic Garside, wrote that the

The mess of No. 14 Squadron made every attempt to make Christmas 1916 as cheerful as possible, staging a pantomime. Here is Captain R. P. Willock (a future air vice-marshal) making a fool of himself in the time-honoured British way – he does not look as if he is enjoying the performance. From The Gnome *of May 1917.* (Author's collection)

pilot, 2nd Lieutenant S. G. Ridley, had shot himself so that his observer could survive to report valuable information. Garside died the day after. Seward heard a rumour that he had murdered Ridley for the water, but this was disproved by Captain Wright of the Imperial Camel Corps, who found the bodies. 'There is no doubt that your boy played the game, and gave the Mechanic another day to hang on to life by leaving him what little water remained and ending his own life', he told Ridley's father.[2] Ridley was twenty.

Yet there was also a light-hearted side to flying over the Sinai. Sometimes, when attempting to intercept enemy reconnaissance planes, Seward would fly up to the front lines in his scout and land, ready to take off as soon as a Hun was spotted. A sergeant pilot accompanied him in a BE2C, its empty observer's cockpit filled with petrol cans so that he could top up his tank and increase his range. It also contained a selection of bottles and, until a German aircraft was sighted, Seward would lie on the sand under a wing drinking champagne. Bottled beer was available for the sergeant pilot.

Many aircrew were very young men, with a distinctly juvenile sense of humour. Large ranges of sand closets had been erected, with canvas partitions but open to the sky. Pilots liked to swoop down on them, pulling out of the dive at the last moment, in the hope that they would be mistaken for German raiders and the occupants would rush out to take cover in the desert with their breeches round their boots. 'Zooming' stopped, however, after a complaint from an infuriated general who had been a victim.

An airman's existence on the Sinai Front had compensations. If food in the mess at Kilo 143 (cooked by Sudanese chefs who wore billowing white robes) was scarcely luxurious and included large quantities of 'bully beef', in bizarre contrast plenty of champagne was drunk in the canvas ante-room before dinner. Pilots could afford it because of their flying pay – by another name, danger money.

They also drank a good deal of spirits to soothe their nerves, especially when the squadron had taken casualties. *The Gnome* recommends 'Blood and Iron':

> The juice of a lemon. A dessertspoonful or more of whisky, double this amount of gin adding two large dashes of Angostura bitters. Two or three large lumps of sugar and fill up with Umbra [mineral water] and ice to the top of a large tumbler. Stir diligently throughout.[3]

Everybody knew that as soon as they took off next morning a hangover would be blown away by the slipstream rushing past an open cockpit – if not, it could be cured by climbing to 8,000 ft.

They generally spent the evenings playing poker or listening to such records as 'Alexander's Ragtime Band' or 'The Kipling Rag' – 'You should see how the foxes trot, all the elephants are wearing dancing shoes', and so on. These records were large Bakelite 78s, played on a clockwork gramophone with a large horn, that needed cranking up over and over again as well as constant changes of the needle. An infallible means of achieving popularity was to bring back a supply of the newest records for the mess after going on leave – returning to the front without at least one was an unforgivable offence.

There was, of course, a piano and a certain amount of singing. One chorus, heard in every RFC Mess, was 'You're only a PBO' – meaning 'Poor Bloody Observer'. It went to the tune of 'A Bachelor Gay', from *The Maid of the Mountains*, the popular London 'show' of the day, and contained the words:

> At seventeen thou. he's shooting rather badly at a Pfalz of tender blue,
> At fifteen thou. you see him point out sadly some Huns of a different hue,
> At ten or twelve he's shooting rather madly at six or eight or more.
> When he fancies he is past hope
> Fires a long burst as a last hope
> And a Hun spins down on fire to the floor!

But the last thing my father would have enjoyed was a singsong.

On the other hand, despite the champagne and the cocktails, living in the Sinai could be horribly uncomfortable. Flies covered the food and had to be beaten off while eating. Snakes – sand vipers and puff-adders – abounded: on one occasion a small sand viper (very like an asp of the sort that killed Cleopatra) slithered into the mess, its back being quickly broken with a swagger stick. Occasionally scorpions hid in field boots when these were removed for the night. Other insect life included large, venomous spiders and centipedes 6 inches long that regularly marched into the tents, while beautiful but foul-smelling scarab beetles crept into bedding. Mosquitoes attacked in singing clouds, horse flies stung more savagely than any in Ireland, sometimes forcing their way into a man's mouth through his lips, and camel flies left one dripping in poisoned blood. A sand-fly bite brought on a fever which, although not a killer, made the victim feel limp and exhausted for days on end.

Sand got into everything, including the meals, despite the best efforts of the Sudanese cooks – and into other places. An infantry officer sent a poem on the subject to *Punch*:

> The sand one meets in Palestine at first will make you wonder where
> The cause is of raspiness apparent in your underwear;
> We've seen a suffering novice after hasting to inspect his hide
> Erroneously indent for half a hogshead of insecticide.

Arms and legs were often 'washed' by rubbing them with sand because water was in such short supply, although it might make the slightest cut, graze, scratch or insect bite turn septic and need medical treatment. (Elastoplast bandages and antibiotics had not yet been invented.) Sand was at its worst in the sandstorms, the *khamsin* – billowing, blinding, scorching fogs of gritty yellow dust that provoked an intolerable thirst.

Yet Seward learned to love the Sinai. The daily renewal of heat and colour at sunrise always seemed to come as a miracle after the cold blackness of the night hours. 'By day the hot sun fermented us; and we were dizzied by the beating wind', wrote Lawrence of his own life in a sandy wilderness. 'At night we were stained by dew, and shamed into pettiness by the innumerable silences of stars.'[4] Neither a poet nor a mystic, my father, too, succumbed to the magic of the desert.

Always a solitary man, never much of a mixer, he spent a lot of time alone with books he bought in Cairo, reading in his tent, although he was in no way what he called a 'beastly, long-haired intellectual'. These were surprisingly

Not many areas in the Sinai yielded water from a pump like this – it was in such short supply that arms and legs often had to be 'washed' with sand, while sometimes even shaving was forbidden. (Author's collection)

serious, including Herodotus, Thucydides, Xenophon, Plutarch and Livy, in Everyman translations. He also waded through Gibbon's *Decline and Fall of the Roman Empire* and Mommsen's *History of Rome*. He did not care much for English fiction apart from Kipling, but enjoyed Alexandre Dumas, Anatole France, Alphonse Daudet and Flaubert (only *Salammbô*), all in French, together with Duruy's *Histoire de France*, which became a favourite. In addition, he read the Koran over and over again – in English, although he was learning Arabic. Among his brother officers, only Freeman shared a taste for serious literature.

Seward soon learned that the only thing an RFC officer in the Sinai could be sure of every morning was that he was going to take his life in his hands. On one occasion his plane refused to come out of a dive and, as the

The Adjutant of No. 14 Squadron, Captain Vaudrey Adolph Albrecht, at home in his tent in the new aerodrome at Kilo 143, spring 1917. (Author's collection)

ground rushed up to meet him, he threw his arms over his face and prayed '*In manus tuas, Domine!*' He was woken by hearing a Tommy say, 'What's that bugger doing up there?', to find his plane had ended up in the branches of a large tree. (Presumably he crashed at an oasis.) Another day, after a fight with a bull-nosed Albatros, he got home safely, to discover that a clip of ammunition in his pocket had two German machine-gun bullets stuck in it – he recalled 'a gentle buffet on the thigh'. He kept the clip for years as a good luck token.

An old-fashioned Catholic in the French way – if in those days of the *croyant* rather than the *pratiquant* sort and seldom at Mass – who normally found the Church of England alien, although it was the religion of his Anglo-Irish ancestors, he nevertheless became deeply impressed by the Anglican burial service, especially by one particular prayer. 'Man that is born of woman hath but a short time to live, and is full of misery. He cometh up and is cut down like a flower: he fleeth as though it were a shadow, and never continueth in one stay. In the midst of life we are in death . . .' He said he knew this prayer by heart after attending so many funerals in the Sinai. The services were always read by the senior officer available since there were no padres.

Accompanied by distinctive, foul-smelling puffs of black, cordite smoke, 'Archie' – from the Austro-Hungarian gunners who were fighting for the Turks – often proved dauntingly effective. Moreover, as cannot be stressed too much, at this stage of the campaign in the Sinai the German planes were faster and better armed; believing in quality rather than quantity, Berlin dispatched the latest models to the Middle East, unlike London which for a long period sent machines that were already six months out of date. Shipped in barges down the Danube to Constantinople, then across the Bosporus and overland to Damascus where they were assembled before a long rail journey to the front, when they arrived these aircraft gave the German fliers a menacing edge, especially over the clumsy BE2Cs that formed the bulk of No. 14 Squadron's aircraft. The Germans thought the BEs so easy to shoot down as to be a joke – 'sehr komisch'.

A rare snap of a Fokker Eindecker *taking off. Armed with a Spandau machine gun firing through the propeller arc, although not so lethal as in France (since there were comparatively few of them) they were much feared in the Sinai during 1916–17. Their preferred method of attack was to dive out of the sun from a blind spot, taking their prey by surprise. After a Fokker had dived, however, if it missed, its rate of climb was so slow that it could never regain height and was at an opponent's mercy. This model is an EIII.* (Philip Jarrett)

For reasons already explained, at this stage of the war there were far fewer dogfights over the Sinai than over the Western Front, although they certainly took place. Contrary to popular belief, they were usually inconclusive – you had to be an experienced, self-confident pilot to take on an enemy aircraft, particularly if it was a better machine than your own. Flying up to engage in a combat of this sort, my father said he always felt scared, trembling and sick in the stomach, slugging brandy from a flask. But, he said, as soon as your plane began to shake when the enemy's bullets started hitting it, you became so angry that all you could think of was downing your opponent, oblivious of everything save manoeuvring and shooting. If you thought you had shot him down – although usually it was impossible to be sure – you felt a marvellous sense of elation. Whatever happened, you flew home drained by the experience.

Pilots took pains to learn skills that might save their lives. Among the best known was the 'Immelmann Turn', devised by a German Fokker ace for use when an enemy plane was close behind. If properly performed, a half loop, then a roll off the top to gain height, could reverse the situation, putting the pilot on his enemy's tail instead. Another was 'side-stepping' – veering away in an imperceptible fraction of a turn when being pursued, so that the enemy's bullets missed. My father explained that this was extremely difficult to do, requiring a great deal of practice and strong nerves, but that it had saved his life more than once.

Some measures were more ingenious than effective. The most 'Heath Robinson' consisted of a machine gun lashed to the bottom of a Jumbo Martinsyde's fuselage, pointing backwards and fired by a lanyard tied to the trigger: a periscope beneath a hole in the bottom of the cockpit supposedly enabled the pilot to see if he was being attacked from below and warned him when to pull the lanyard. According to my father, there was no record of the device having had any success.

More Fokker monoplanes reached the Sinai Front, regularly ambushing machines. Some pilots stopped wearing goggles as they prevented them seeing out of the corners of their eyes. The thing to remember, my father said, when an *Eindecker* pounced on you from some blind spot was that it could never regain height, as its rate of climb was so slow – under-powered, it was hard to fly. If you evaded the initial attack, easy enough in a Bristol Scout, although difficult in an unwieldy BE2C or Jumbo Martinsyde, then you usually regained the initiative – provided you watched out for an Immelmann turn. But a Fokker was nearly always able to escape by diving away.

WELS's flying helmet and goggles, replacements bought in London during the summer of 1917 for those lost after being shot down. (Author's collection)

The Germans attacked Kilo 143 several times. On one occasion Seward was trying to take off in his little Bristol Scout to fight the enemy in the air when the mechanic whose job it was to swing the propeller in order to start the machine panicked. 'Oh my God, they're coming down on us! They're coming down on us!' he screamed as the bombs began to fall. My father, who was a

sitting duck, had to switch the engine off and yell for a sergeant to put the man under arrest and find someone else to swing the propeller. Bombs were dropping all around his plane before he eventually got off the ground.

Quite apart from the hazards of Archie fire, or bombs, or being outgunned by a superior enemy machine, the RFC's wood and canvas aircraft were tricky to fly, failing even the most experienced pilots. 'She's like some breeds of car – you want to be a mechanical genius to understand her ... but she's often been nearly the death of me',[5] is how Buchan makes one of his airmen speak of a notoriously temperamental type of machine in *Mr Standfast*. Some planes could turn into death traps, especially when they went into a spin. Even the simplest manoeuvre was perilous, while Seward recalled that, 'Taking off and landing, that was the most dangerous.' Members of No. 14 Squadron were frequently in hospital after being pulled out from the wreckage – if they were lucky.

As on the Western Front, both British and German pilots on the Palestine Front flew without parachutes. Although this was partly due to the 'Powers that Be' considering them bad for morale, it was also because the art of packing them had not been perfected. ('Balloonatics' simply slung them from the side of their observation baskets.) Even so, a few experiments were made at fitting them on planes, outside the cockpit. According to Seward, during one of these experiments an intrepid parachutist was dragged along the entire length of a Jewish battalion's main latrine trench.

There were no illuminated dashboards for flying after dark. Nor were there any floodlights, night-time landing strips being marked by two lines of crude flares made from half-empty petrol cans into which lighted matches had been dropped. Seward recalled with horror the dreadful burns suffered by a brother officer, Campbell-Robertson, when he lit one of these 'flares' downwind.

Pilots disliked flying at what for those days were high altitudes, even if it reduced the chances of being attacked by enemy aircraft. Unlike the Western Front, there was comparatively little fighting high up. When you reached 15,000 ft the temperature dropped below 15 °F, which in an open canvas cockpit was almost unbearable. Protective clothing consisted only of a leather

Left: Stuart Reid in typical flying gear of the period. At this stage of the war pilots generally dressed like this, in very light helmets, long leather overcoats and field boots – clothing that was a bit too warm at low altitudes and not much protection against the cold at high ones. November 1916. (Author's collection)

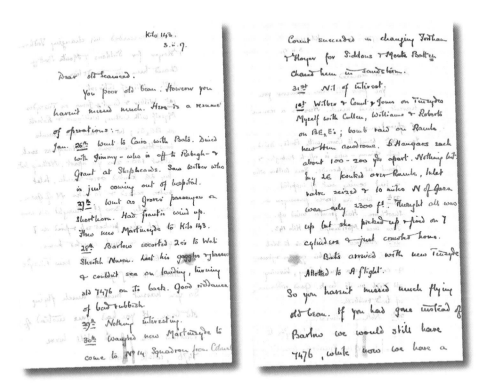

Pages from Freeman's letter of 3 February 1917 to 'Seaweed'. (Author's collection)

overcoat, a leather helmet – more of a cap than a helmet – gauntlets and rudimentary 'smoked-glass' goggles with a bit of fur round the edges. Flying boots did not exist until well on into the war so that airmen flew in knee-high military field boots (laced over the instep) or ankle boots with leather gaiters. Oxygen supplies were not yet available and you became light-headed at a surprisingly low height.

But since machines normally operated at a fairly low altitude, in such a warm climate aircrew often dispensed with leather overcoats. (This explains why No. 14 Squadron's captured pilots, Floyer and Palmer, are wearing uniforms in the photograph taken by their German hosts.) If it was particularly hot weather, they flew in shirtsleeves and shorts.

Towards the end of 1916 Seward was laid up in hospital, recovering from a twisted knee after a crash – an injury that plagued him until the day he died. While recuperating, he received a letter from his friend Freeman at Kilo 143, dated 3 February 1917, which he kept for the rest of his life. Almost a page from a war diary, it is worth quoting in full:

Dear old Seaweed,

You poor old bean. You haven't missed much. Here is a resumé of operations.

Jan. 26th. Went to Cairo with Bats [Page ?]. Dined with Jimmy – who is off to Rabegh [with the flight sent to help Lawrence] – and Grant at Shepheards. Saw Wilber [Willock] who is just coming out of hospital.

27th. Went as Groves' passenger on Shorthorn. Had frantic wind up. Flew new Martinsyde to Kilo 143.

28th. Barlow escorted [BE]2Cs to Weli Sheikh Nuran. Lost his goggles and glasses and couldn't see on landing, turning old 7476 on its back. Good riddance of bad rubbish.

29th. Nothing interesting.

30th. Wangled new Martinsyde to come to No. 14 Squadron from Colonel. Count [Albrecht] succeeded in changing Fordham and Floyer for Siddons and Moute Batten [?].

Chased here in sandstorm.

31st. Nil of interest.

1st [Feb.] Wilber and [the] Count and Jones on Tinsydes. Myself with Cullen, Williams and Roberts on BE2Es; bomb raid on Ramle [sic]. New Hun aerodrome. 6 hangars each about 100–200 yards apart. Nothing hit. My 2E konked out over Ramle, inlet valve seized and 10 miles N of Gaza was only 2,300 feet. Thought all was up but she picked up and fired on 7 cylinders and just crawled home.

Bats arrived with new Tinsyde. Alloted to A flight.

So you haven't missed much flying, old bean. If you had gone instead of Barlow we would still have 7476, while now we have a good new one. By the time you come out of hospital Fordham and Floyer will be here and probably the Count will have another Tinsyde. Your turn will come, old bean, but just at present we have myself and Count, Kingsley – when he returns – Fordham and Wilber, so you, Barlow and Floyer will only be getting short flights until we get more machines I'm afraid; or until some of us leave the squadron.

Your letter only arrived today, so it took 5 days to come here. Don't worry about your old knee and let it heal up as it wants. The more you

worry the longer it will take. You're certain to get your go on Tinsydes
in time and for the present Barlow is not getting very much, especially
in this bad weather.

So long old bean and let us know when to expect you.

Love from all

H. R. Freeman[6]

The weather in January 1917 had been very bad indeed, with bursts of
heavy rain accompanied by fierce gales. In addition, there were several vicious
sandstorms, and not just the one mentioned by Freeman. This made flying
unusually difficult, resulting in more than one crash. Even so, the Squadron
had continued to operate, being grounded on only a few exceptionally
dangerous days.

Seward was back on active service within a few days and given a Bristol
Scout, always his favourite aircraft. He then experienced what he regarded as
one of the most interesting moments of his life. In a letter of February 1967,
he wrote a short account:

> Fifty years ago – in February 1917 – I was on hostile aircraft patrol
> between El Arish and the Dead Sea when I spotted two German
> reconnaissance planes, probably Rumplers, and tried to cut them
> off from their aerodrome at Ramle. However, they flew east instead
> towards the Mountains of Moab, where they may have known of a
> landing ground, and being faster than my own Bristol Scout, managed
> to escape.
>
> During the pursuit I noticed a promontory at the eastern end of the
> Dead Sea with remains of ancient fortifications, but unfortunately I
> was prevented from returning to take a closer look by a lack of fuel.
> Later I passed over it on several flights.
>
> My squadron included a keen amateur archaeologist, Major Harold
> Freeman, who told me that this was Masada and lent me a copy of
> Josephus, since when I have always been fascinated by the fortress
> and its story. Were Freeman and I the first men to fly over Masada?
> Freeman may have known, but I never asked him and a few months
> later he was shot down in flames on the Western Front.[7]

Masada was the last stronghold of the Jewish Zealots who fought on after
the Romans had destroyed Jerusalem in AD 70. Besieged by the legionaries

Freeman flying a BE2C, snapped from the front cockpit by WELS who was acting as his observer – so many machines broke down and were out of service that the pilots of single-seaters often filled this role. Some experienced airmen always flew without goggles to avoid restricting their field of vision and minimise the risk of ambush by enemy aircraft. Freeman's tense expression shows he is on the look-out for an attack – perhaps suspecting there may be a Fokker above him, waiting to pounce. Early 1917. (Author's collection)

and after a heroic defence, the entire garrison with their families – nearly a thousand souls – committed mass suicide rather than surrender, inspired by a magnificent speech made by their commander. The story is known only from the Jewish historian Flavius Josephus. Freeman lent Seward a copy of Whiston's translation of Josephus' *The Wars of the Jews*, a book he read and re-read almost until the day he died.

Shortly after this, the squadron at Kilo 143 had a run of bad luck. Lieutenant A. J. Barlow failed to return from patrol on 15 February and – as has been discussed – Lieutenants Floyer and Palmer did the same on 5 March. Like the last two, Barlow survived and was given a chivalrous welcome by the Germans. The fact that the three survived unscathed suggests they had been forced down, something that official records were always loath to admit. In *Mr Standfast* Buchan describes a surrender in mid-air: 'Sloping down in wide circles came a German machine, and, following a little behind and a little above, a British.'[8] (This was a sight Buchan may have witnessed on the Western Front with his own eyes.)

Another guest of Fliegerabteilung 300. Lt A. J. Barlow with an Austrian officer and
German officers in Turkish uniform, 15 February 1917. As always, the 'Huns' gave him
'a damned good lunch' in their mess at Beersheba. From The Gnome, *May 1917.*
(Author's collection)

The latest German scout was what my father and his friends in the Sinai
called the 'bull-nosed' Albatros, because its cigar-shaped, plywood fuselage
resembled a popular Morris motor car of the day. (It was more generally known
among the RFC in France as an 'Albatros Vee-Strutter', from the V-shaped
struts joining the upper and lower wings.) On the Western Front the Albatros
DIII was responsible for the high casualty rate among the RFC during spring
1917 that gave 'Bloody April' its name. It was enviably nippy, no bigger than
a Martinsyde and well armed, its twin, synchronized Spandau guns firing
through the propeller arc were capable of blasting an opponent into shreds.

The most formidable of the pilots flying these machines in Palestine was
Oberleutnant Gerhard Felmy, a cheerful Berliner in his twenties. The brother
of Fliegerabteilung 300's new commander, Hauptmann Hellmuth Felmy, he
was a regular soldier, a former infantry officer who had joined the German
Army in 1910. On one occasion, flying an Albatros DIII, he attacked a BE2C

escorted by No. 14 Squadron's sole DH1 and nearly shot down the redoubtable pusher, damaging its propeller and tailplane. If scarcely the Richthofen of the Sinai, the Oberleutnant had several kills to his credit; reports from Turkish military headquarters often mention his exploits. Every flyer on the Palestine Front, British and Australian as well as his comrades, admired Gerhard Felmy, who embodied the old school of German chivalry. The welcome given to Floyer, Palmer and Barlow would be repeated some months later when Felmy downed an Australian airman.

The editor of *The Gnome*, Dixon-Spain, was deeply moved by this sort of behaviour, 'that something of romance and chivalry which seems to be only found nowadays in the air', he wrote in his little paper in January 1917. 'It is quaint that this ancient tradition should, as it were, relive in the last word of scientific warfare.' Although nothing quite like it was taking place in France, where the unending death grapple made good manners difficult, he cited an example from another front, reprinting an article from the American *Daily News*. It had been written by a special correspondent who had visited the single RFC squadron in Mesopotamia during August the previous year:

'The British Aviators trust that the German pilot of the Fokker aeroplane which was shot down yesterday was neither seriously injured or killed.'

This note was penned in English after a two hours wrangle in the Aviation Camp as to its phraseology and whether it should be in bad German or good English. There was not one dissenter from the spirit of the note. The message was sealed up in a long canvas bag and dropped into the Turkish Lines addressed to 'The German Aviators'.

The note was in return for a great courtesy. Some time ago a British aeroplane tumbled to the earth behind the Turkish Lines. Both pilot and observer were killed. A few days later a canvas-bound package was dropped into the British Aerodrome from a Turkish Aeroplane. Safely packed between two pillows were two watches, two cigarette cases, a ring and some other trinkets with a letter which in effect said, 'The German Aviators with the Turkish Army regret the sad death of two very gallant hostile aviators. They return the personal effects of these brave men thinking that perhaps their mothers would like to have them.'

Who says there is no chivalry in modern war?[9]

An Albatros DIII, captured in the Middle East. Exceptionally manoeuvrable and armed with twin Spandau machine guns, the 'bull-nosed' Albatros had been responsible for the slaughter of countless RFC pilots during 'Bloody April' 1917 on the Western Front – where for some months it was Richthofen's favourite plane. It became much feared in the Sinai, especially when flown by a man like Gerhard Felmy. (Philip Jarrett)

(When the RFC occupied the aerodrome at Baghdad in March 1917, they found painted on a wrecked Albatros the message, 'With kind regards to our British comrades, [from] the German airmen. "God save the King!"')

The enemy's treatment of his brother officers made Seward think better of them. In any case, he saw human beings in terms of class rather than race. He could find little reason to hate the Germans whom he was fighting, admiring their courage. He never called them 'Huns'. Afterwards, he said that, while at the time he loathed the idea, it might have been no bad thing for France if the Germans had won the Battle of the Marne, since it would have put an end to the Third Republic and perhaps just possibly brought back the monarchy – the French were 'never any good without a king or an emperor'. And it would have saved the world from Hitler.

What he particularly disliked was the sort of hysterical xenophobia that was making the British abuse people with German names or kick dachshunds. He would have thoroughly agreed with an editorial in *The Gnome* of August

1917 that referred to the shameful 'yelling in the ½d. Press' for blood reprisals against Germany because of its air raids on London. The editorial continued:

> The Archbishop of Canterbury has said that he has been inundated with letters on his opposition to air raid reprisals. 'What has startled and horrified me', said His Grace, 'is the kind of way in which a number of people are regarding this question. I ventured to say in a letter that if we had dead babies in the streets of London it did not surely make us feel that we wanted to see dead babies in the streets of Germany or elsewhere. I got letters from people who did not keep their names back to say that was exactly what we do want. "We want to see the streets run red with blood, and women and children reduced to pulp." This is the kind of phrase which has, I am afraid, found currency, not I hope and believe to a very large extent, in the country, but at all events it betokens a growth of something which I believe would not have been said or thought a little time ago.'
>
> We quite agree with the Archbishop. Outbreaks of this sort are contemptible, probably the result of panic fear. If all this ferocity could be imported into the fighting line it might be useful – but it is eminently the sort of thing which increases as the square of the distance from danger. We confess to a recent disquietude at the apparent growth of 'prussianized' ideas among officers with whom we have been in contact. It's not a great thing: it takes the form of arguing for atrocities which the disputant knows full well could never be acquiesced in fact. It is, nevertheless, something very different to the old army ideal, and something which has recently crept in.[10]

Notes

1. 'Operations Record Book, No. 14 (Bombing) Squadron', p. 2.
2. Letter from Ridley's father, quoting Captain Wright, in documentation concerning *The Ridley Tragedy* at the Department of Art, Imperial War Museum, London.
3. *The Gnome*, January 1917, p. 16.
4. T. E. Lawrence, *Seven Pillars of Wisdom*, p. 27.
5. J. Buchan, *Mr Standfast*, p. 337.
6. WELS Archive.
7. *Ibid.*
8. Buchan, *Mr Standfast*, p. 380.
9. *The Gnome*, January 1917, p. 8.
10. *The Gnome*, August 1917, pp. 1–2.

CHAPTER 5

LEAVE IN CAIRO

**'It would be idle to suggest that young men of high
spirits could sustain their hours of ease with
monkish contemplation.'**

W. Raleigh and H. A. Jones, **The War in the Air**

There was plenty of local leave. Just as officers on the Western Front swiftly travelled back from the trenches to London's restaurants and 'shows', those on the Middle Eastern Front left the desert for the delights of Cairo, which was only a short train and ferry ride away from El Arish. At that time one of the pleasure capitals of the world, another Monte Carlo, with five great hotels and a climate superior to that of the Riviera, it catered for every imaginable fleshly indulgence.

The Germans (whose own places of relaxation were Damascus or Constantinople which took weeks to reach along the primitive Ottoman railway) felt so jealous that once – only once, since Cairo had plenty of planes to defend it – they sent a Zeppelin to bomb the place, the sole victim being an unfortunate lady walking her dog. On another occasion, in November 1916, a single German aircraft dropped some small bombs, which killed a British soldier and a dozen Egyptian civilians, besides wounding a score of others. Apart from these two raids, no city could have felt further removed from hostilities.

Until 1914, Egypt had been part of the Ottoman Empire in theory, although in reality it was occupied by Britain. When Turkey entered the war, Britain announced that the country had become a 'British protectorate', replacing the pro-Turkish *khedive* (viceroy) by his more malleable uncle whom they proclaimed sultan, while in 1916 they imposed martial law – on the unlikely pretext that the Egyptians might rise in favour of Turkey. As a consequence, Britain's control of the capital was absolute and its troops felt as if they belonged to a master race.

A newly built railway ran from El Arish to Ismailia, where you took a barge across the Canal and then boarded another train to Cairo. Seward's first visit

Officers of No. 14 Squadron off to Cairo on leave. Spring 1917. (Author's collection)

was soon after he joined the Squadron, during the second half of October 1916. On a postcard to his mother he says that he found Ghiza 'simply lovely' and enjoyed going round the bazaars in the 'native quarter'.

The flesh pots of Cairo, some very wicked indeed, flourished as never before, the eager troops being fleeced in delightful bars and eating places, and in enticing brothels. The most popular hotel among the military was the legendary Shepheard's in Sharia Kamel, only five minutes from the station, with 350 bedrooms, the cheapest of which cost 40 piastres a night – about 9s. Set in beautiful tropical gardens, as well as a vast restaurant it had a grill room, an American bar, ballrooms and billiard rooms – the wrought-iron balcony, running along the front of the building, where a band played every afternoon, provided a grandstand from where guests could watch the colourful 'natives'. During the war the hotel was taken over by British officers, who regularly ate there – exuberantly celebrating the slightest victory. It soon became a home from home for Eric Seward, as it did for every member of No. 14 Squadron.

However, he seldom breakfasted at Shepheard's – always, in his own words, a *'fine fourchette'* – preferring to go out and do so on coffee and a caviare sandwich at Groppi's Coffee House. This was a sham rococo building that looked very like something from a Paris boulevard, with tall windows, luxurious, high-ceilinged rooms and display galleries, situated in Chareh el Manakh (later Suleiman Pasha Square). It was also a very high-class grocery, specializing in exotic delicacies and fine wines. Groppi's was where No. 14 Squadron ordered its champagne. It still survives today.

There was a vigorous social life. Cocktail parties, dinner parties and dances were laid on by British residents for young officers on leave from the desert, although, irritatingly, members of Murray's staff tended to monopolize the girls. There were also some excellent clubs and Seward appears to have been a (temporary) member of at least two. One was the Cairo Turf Club, a comparatively small building that stood next to the Sephardi synagogue in Maghreby Street and possessed a famous bar. The other was the Gezira Sporting Club amid its lilac groves on the island of Gezira, near the former botanical gardens. This had a golf course, squash and tennis courts, polo grounds and a race course for both flat racing and steeplechasing, with a fine grandstand. Seward enjoyed the racing, having an exceptionally good eye for a horse, always betting on the tote.

The officers' usual transport to the Canal on leave was a Crossley tender. Spring 1917. (Author's collection)

Shepheard's Hotel, Cairo, which became a home from home for British officers on leave from the Sinai Desert and Palestine. Their behaviour after dinner was frequently uproarious and did not endear them to the local population. (Author's collection)

He also liked to visit the newly built Museum of Antiquities near the Kasr-el-Nil bridge, purchasing one or two 'genuine *ushabiti* [funerary figures]' at its *salle de vente*. The museum consolidated what was to be a lasting love affair with ancient Egypt that had begun with his reading Herodotus.

My father once confided in me, however, that his favourite places of relaxation in Cairo had been the brothels. The city contained houses of ill fame to suit every taste and purse, many of the prostitutes being Italian, although the madams were usually French. He frequented the more expensive sort, all red plush, potted palms, art-nouveau bronzes and mildly erotic prints from *La Vie Parisienne*, with a melancholy man ceaselessly playing a grand piano – the tunes were lugubrious renderings of Verdi's fruitier arias or of French music-hall songs, such as 'Frou-Frou', 'Madelon' or 'La Belle Tonkinoise'. He carefully explained to me that he was drawn to these establishments not by the staff but by the management, the madams, who held court in cosy little drawing rooms, the best-informed people in the city, to whom he enjoyed chatting in French. Bordellos like this existed all over the Turkish world.

J.GROPPI

11, Chareh el Manakh
CAIRO

Undertakes to
supply all orders
in any direction
either by Post
parcels or accel
erated Goods

CAKES + CHOCOLATE
CONFECTIONERY
PRESERVES + WINES
SPIRITS

packing most carefully
superintended

Henry Wybrow & Cᵒ

HIGH CLASS
MILITARY TAILORS

Breeches Specialists

PERFECT FIT GUARANTEED

19, Chareh el Manakh
::   CAIRO   ::

M. AVATIS

LONDON AGENTS
W. H. SMITH & SON

BOOKSELLER. . . . .
STATIONER . . . . . .
AND NEWSAGENT

LARGE ASSORTMENT OF BOOKS IN
VARIOUS CHEAP EDITIONS BY THE
::   MOST POPULAR AUTHORS.   ::

BOOKS ON FLIGHT
BOOKS ON EGYPT
BOOKS ON THE WAR

BEST ASSORTMENT OF STATIONERY
AT REASONABLE PRICES

BRANCH BOOKSHOPS AT
CAIRO, ALEXANDRIA, ISMAILIA, SUEZ.

An advertisement for Groppi's, the famous Parisian-style café and luxury grocers which supplied champagne to No. 14 Squadron's mess, where it was consumed in large quantities – despite problems of refrigeration in the desert. When on leave in Cairo, WELS invariably breakfasted here rather than at Shepheard's Hotel, always on coffee and a caviare sandwich. From The Gnome, *March 1917.* (Author's collection)

A friend, shot down over Syria, managed to reach one such haven in Damascus where he lived happily for an entire year, the madam accepting Cox's Bank cheques in payment – and finding no trouble in cashing them – before he escaped to the Piraeus inside the propeller shaft of a Greek cargo boat.

Seward had no need to patronize whores despite his battered face, since he was never without a girlfriend, due to some sort of animal magnetism apparent only to the other sex. He also had a musical, unusually attractive voice that was one of the pleasantest I ever heard in a man and, if he wanted, could summon up great charm for women, whom he adored – he was what Frenchmen call *'un homme à femmes'*. His attitude of amused chivalry towards them would raise more than a few eyebrows among today's feminist circles, however. 'Never lose your temper with girls when they're late', he was accustomed to say. 'The poor things can't help it.'

A peculiarly unpleasant relationship existed between the British and better-educated Egyptians, who naturally enough sympathized with their fellow Muslims, the Turks, privately referring to their city as 'Cairo the Neutral'. Egyptian culture was basically Ottoman, and Constantinople hoped, somewhat optimistically, that Egypt would rise against the British, which was one reason why they attacked the Suez Canal. Awareness of this sympathy did not endear the 'Gippies', as they were known, to their new rulers. Admittedly, Britain tried to govern more gently than the former Turkish-style regime. No longer did a native swing from each of the four corners of a house in which a European had been found murdered, while life was probably safer, justice fairer, taxes lighter and education more available than in the old days. Yet Egyptian resentment at being a British dependency grew steadily, voiced by such eloquent politicians as Zaghlul Pasha.

The wild antics of drunken young officers embittered the relationship still further. Among these were after-dinner races in gharries (horse-drawn cabs) or the game of 'boarders away' – which meant jumping on board a horse-drawn bus, making the driver go at full speed by threatening him with a swagger stick and then forcing all the Egyptian passengers to jump off. Other ranks, especially the Australians, behaved with even more brutality, shooting up bars and eating-houses.

Perhaps surprisingly in the circumstances, there seem to have been a few Egyptians who actually liked the British. Some of the younger even admired the RFC, and at least one 'Gippy' aspired to join it, as can be seen from a letter printed in *The Gnome*:

Sir,

I have the honour to inform yourself by this application that, as I am an Egyptian man, of eighteen years old, and latin Catholic's religion, I wish to engage myself volontairy at the Royal Flying Corps as pupil's aviator.

I am employed at the National Bank of Egypt, and I shall leave my employ, when my application shall be accepted to serve bravely and with joy the Great British Army.

In the hope of a favourable reply,

I am, Sir,

Your faithfull servant

A_____ C_____ [1]

Nevertheless, Seward 'made friends' with one or two Egyptian ladies, so that he could practise his Arabic. He recalled happily that 'beneath their robes, everything came from Paris and they even wore Poiret shoes.' (Poiret shoes were then the height of Parisian chic.) He also had quite a number of Arab acquaintances of whom he saw a good deal, but these were invariably Syrians. He also liked the Sudanese, 'marvellous servants and bloody good soldiers'.

Yet he learned to enjoy the real, non-European Cairo, in those days still a medieval city from the Arabian Nights, wandering through its narrow streets, peering into mosques and Coptic churches. He acquired a genuine regard for the Copts, who had steadfastly refused to abandon their ancient form of Christianity despite living under Muslim rule since AD 642, and who still worshipped in the language of the pharaohs.

Above all, he became fascinated by Egyptology, more or less hero-worshipping Sir Flinders Petrie – the fashionable archaeologist of the day – and reading all his books from cover to cover. On a postcard he describes how, in November 1916, he and a friend from the Squadron (Freeman?) had just visited a place near the Pyramids 'where tourists never go', without the distraction of a guide. 'We came across dozens of tombs – just a hole in the ground about three feet square. We scrambled into a number and found passages inside, large rooms and lots of inscriptions. Very exciting.'[2]

On average, local leave for RFC officers seems to have been only two full days, which was just enough for the gaiety and glittering indulgence of Cairo to whet the appetite. Then they had to return to the hot sand and the fly-infested tents of Kilo 143.

Stuart Reid off-duty at Ismailia, chatting to local talent. (Despite their veils, many of these Egyptian ladies' clothes would have come straight from Paris.) November, 1916. (Author's collection)

And go back to nightmares of an unthinkable yet all too likely death in the near future, dreams that haunted Seward through the night so that he awoke sweating with a fear he could never admit. He knew it might come without warning, perhaps from going into an uncontrollable spin that ended only when the plane finally corkscrewed into the ground. Or from a machine breaking up so that the crew fell to earth from a very great height, with plenty of time to think about what was coming. Or, most likely of all, from being roasted alive in a flying bonfire.

These were not just morbid fantasies – every airman on both sides had seen too many of his friends die in such ways. If they would not talk about their fear, occasionally the RFC sang a mournful little ditty in their messes, composed by some anonymous bard:

> Every little while my engine's conking,
> Every little while I catch on fire.
> All the time I've got my switch up
> I've always got the wind up,
> Every, every, little while.

However enjoyable, leave in Cairo could only be a short-lived palliative that he might never enjoy again.

Notes

1. *The Gnome*, March 1917, p. 13.
2. 27 November 1916, WELS Archive.

CHAPTER 6

LAWRENCE OF ARABIA

**'. . . bundles of nerves, who to punish themselves
did outrageous things.'**

T. E. Lawrence on RFC pilots, **Seven Pillars of Wisdom**

Within three months Seward acquired a working knowledge of Arabic and
his habit of talking to natives in their own tongue did not go unnoticed.
Late in October 1916 he was offered command of a flight being sent to Yenbo
on the Red Sea, where the Arab army was based. Its job would be to help
Colonel T. E. Lawrence, adviser to the Arab Revolt's military leader, Feisal, the
son of the Sherif of Mecca. Although it meant promotion, my father declined.
'I simply couldn't see any future in it', he explained long afterwards, without
regret. He might have added that he had mixed feelings about Lawrence. In
the event, his place was taken by another Arabic-speaker, Captain A. J. Ross.

No. 14 Squadron and No. 1 Squadron are best known to historians for helping
Lawrence with his Arab Revolt against the Ottoman Empire, in which he tied
down large numbers of Turkish troops, disrupted railways and telegraphs, and
thoroughly humiliated his opponents. No one can deny Lawrence's bravery or
question his genius as a guerrilla leader. Yet while the airmen admired him, he
made them feel oddly uncomfortable.

Surprisingly, there is no mention of Lawrence by name in No. 14 Squadron's
war diary. The sole references to him I can find in it are when flights were
seconded to help his campaign, and then only the flight and its destination
are listed. Although the squadrons admired what he was trying to do, it is not
impossible he made the same impression on them that he made on General
Allenby, Murray's replacement. In *Seven Pillars of Wisdom*, Lawrence himself
says that when he first met Allenby, the new Commander-in-Chief, he 'could
not make out how much was genuine performer and how much charlatan'.
Commenting on this strange admission, Wavell wrote that Allenby 'always
suspected a strong streak of the charlatan in Lawrence'.[1]

Yet the airmen went in awe of Lawrence, as can be seen from the interest they
took in his German counterpart, Wilhelm Wassmuss, who was doing the same

Colonel T. E. Lawrence. Even if WELS thought Lawrence was a hero, he described him as 'the most insignificant-looking little fellow you ever saw, but always very pleasant', while he could never understand why he was so fond of the Bedouin. Because of his ability to speak Arabic, WELS was offered command of the flight sent to Yenbo to help Lawrence, but declined. (London Library)

sort of work for the other side. The Kaiser's consul in Iran, he has been called 'The Lawrence of Persia'. A mystic who loved the desert, dressing in flowing robes and dispensing large sums of gold sent to him from Berlin, he persuaded several nomad tribes to fight the British. General Townshend's surrender at Kut el Amara in 1916 owed something to his activities, while in April 1917 he was described as 'busy in the mountains forty miles away [from Muscat], stirring up local talent against us with no little success'.[2] Britain offered £100,000 in sovereigns for his capture. He remains an obscure figure, however, since he lacked Lawrence's literary skills and talent for legend-building.

Lawrence did not make any friends in No. 14 Squadron. Their names are absent from his letters. In *Seven Pillars of Wisdom*, his highly romantic account of his revolt, he has little to say about the many officers to whom he owed a great deal, save for a few polite references to Major Ross and his successor Captain Stent. He was a bit more interested in Ross Smith from No. 1 Squadron, but because he was an Australian, belonging to a people whom he had not so far encountered. Admittedly, in his slightly inhuman way, he did at least appreciate the courage of the pilots who were constantly risking their lives in fragile, unreliable aircraft. Eating with these young men in their mess, he sensed the terror beneath their bravery – perceptively calling them 'bundles of nerves'.

Once or twice, he refers to Biffy Borton as a dependable officer who had been a great help. Otherwise, he does not mention him, although, as the commander of 5th Wing, Borton decided what planes should be sent to the Arabs' assistance. (Ironically, when Biffy was Commandant of RAF Cranwell, he got to know Lawrence much better as Aircraftsman Ross.[3]) The one person in No. 14 Squadron who may have made some sort of impression on Colonel Lawrence was Stuart Reid, even though Lawrence does not mention him. As a painter, Reid knew how to flatter the hero's vanity and was allowed to portray Lawrence mounted on a racing camel – a picture that has disappeared. He was also to paint Lawrence's awe-struck warriors joyfully greeting a big Handley Page bomber as it stood among smaller machines.

However, the Squadron's association with Lawrence must have been much closer than he suggests. He told John Buchan that he was 'four times in an air crash',[4] some of which can only have been in No. 14 Squadron's machines. According to my father (who also said he 'gave him a lift' several times, presumably in a BE2C), he dined in No. 14's mess at Ismailia quite often, as well as at Kilo 143 later, which means that the connection dated from before he went to Yenbo. No doubt, he was flown from Ismailia to Cairo, to visit General Murray at his headquarters in the Savoy Hotel.

If Seward gave Lawrence a lift two or three times, then so must other pilots. This implies that he consulted General Murray and General Allenby more frequently than he admits in the *Seven Pillars of Wisdom*, which is written as a personal saga; presumably the author does not want to detract from his portrait of himself as a lonely hero by confessing he has been in regular contact with headquarters. It is probable that the RFC brought him more logistic support than he bothers to mention – guns and ammunition, medicine and money. A constant need to obtain these would explain why he spent so many nights at Ismailia or El Arish, and why he dined in the mess so often.

'The most insignificant looking little fellow you ever saw, but always very pleasant, even if he never said much', was how Seward described Lawrence. He did not notice what John Buchan detected, 'his eye which could have made, or quelled, a revolution'.[5] What members of No. 14 Squadron did notice was that, while eating with them in the mess, their guest never bothered to brush away the flies covering his hands, unlike everybody else – 'just as if he had been a bloody Bedu'. However uneasy he made his hosts, he

WELS in a BE2C, still the RFC's workhorse until the end of 1917. Its backward-firing single Lewis gun was so badly sited amid a tangle of brace-wires as to be almost impossible to use. This made the aircraft virtually indefensible, especially when flown as a single-seater (as it is here) in order to carry heavy bombs. In France the BE2C's high casualty rate earned it the grim name of 'Fokker Fodder'. T. E. Lawrence was a frequent passenger in an aircraft of this sort. (Author's collection)

inspired fascination. There were rumours that he spied on the German fliers at Beersheba, disguising himself as a waiter to overhear their conversations.

In one of Lawrence's few references to No. 14 Squadron, he writes that Major Ross, who brought the flight to Yenbo, 'spoke Arabic so adeptly and was so splendid a leader that there could be no two minds as to the wise direction of his help'.[6] He tells us that Ross brought with him four British aeroplanes, BE[2C] machines, and later mentions him as having done sterling work at Rabigh. But that is all.

In fact, accompanied by a company of the Bedford Regiment, in October a flight from No. 14 Squadron had already been dispatched by ship from Suez to Rabigh – further south along the Red Sea from Yenbo, and commanding the route from Medina to Mecca. This was quickly withdrawn for fear the presence of Christians near so holy a Muslim shrine might upset the sensibilities of the Sherif of Mecca. 'Growing Arab fears of a Turkish attack on Mecca by way of Rabigh, however, ovecame the political or religious

A Bedu in about 1916. Many nomads like this spied for the Turks while some fought against the British under German officers, as at the Battle of Romani, although not after it became clear that Turkey was going to be defeated. Since they often stripped and robbed British aircrew who fell into their hands after forced landings in the desert, charging a fee of 50 sovereigns to return them to British lines, they were deeply disliked by the RFC – No. 14 Squadron was astonished by Lawrence's hero-worship of these wild people. (Author's collection)

objections to British aeroplanes', the authors of *The War in the Air* comment drily.[7] On 13 November, commanded by Ross, another flight of six aircraft – not four, as Lawrence says – was landed at Yenbo, this time escorted by a force of about 600 Egyptian troops who brought artillery. The mechanics were so scared of being attacked as unbelievers by the natives that they serviced the planes with rifles stacked at their side. However, the Arabs were delighted that such wonderful machines had come to their aid – they called them 'Tiyaras', which meant 'female flying things'.

Sending a flight to Yenbo was not the only help given by No. 14 Squadron to Lawrence at this stage. On 24 November 1916, together with Lieutenant S. K. Muir of No. 1 Squadron, Harold Freeman made a gallant attempt to cut the Hejaz railway. In Martinsydes, they flew from Mustabig in the Sinai and back, a round trip of 350 miles that took them five hours, which at this date was incredible. Freeman dived on a railway bridge near Qal'at el Hasa, dropping two 100-lb delayed-action bombs from 20 ft, one of which hit the bridge but bounced off, although doing considerable damage to the railway line itself.

Muir was also unlucky in failing to score a direct hit when he attacked the station at Jurf ed Derawish. 'The visibility was phenomenal and, from one point, the whole of the Dead Sea, a strip of the Mediterranean, and a part of the Red Sea, were available from the aeroplanes.'[8] It was Freeman, always a romantic, who put this on record. 'This attack was made with a twofold object', explains the war diary. 'First, to demonstrate to the Arabs who had not yet joined in the Hejaz revolt the wide range of our power; and secondly to assist the rebel Arabs by handicapping the Turks in Medina, whose sole line of supply was by this railway.'[9]

Yet the Turks continued to advance and by December were threatening Yenbo and Rabigh. Ross kept watch on their movements, photographing their positions, from small airstrips at both places. On 10 December the Turks were within only 6 miles of Yenbo. Seaplanes of the RNAS, operating from HMS *Raven II*, bombed and machine-gunned the enemy, which helped to stop them from coming any nearer. Ross's planes continued to fly from Rabigh until March 1917, even photographing Turkish positions in front of Medina. On 5 March a British aircraft flew over Medina for the first time and took photographs, but because Medina is sacred it did not drop bombs. It encountered three German machines over the city but made no attempt at interception.

In mid-March Ross moved his base from Yenbo to the newly captured Wehj. Since his object was to bomb the Hejaz railway in as many places as possible, most of them out of range, it was necessary for him to build a number of advanced landing strips. In the waterless desert this was not an easy business as the temperature in the shade could sometimes be as high as 112°F. The Arabs helped by recommending likely sites. Such a message from the Emir Ali is recorded in *The War in the Air*: 'Respected Major Ross, we should prefer your coming out to us to inspect the spot we are about to select as an alighting place for your aeroplanes. Accordingly, we have sent to you Dakhl Bin Talal and Atiya Bin Muheisin that you may set forth in their company to us. Moreover, they have with them a trotting she-camel for your mount. We await you at Bir Abbas. Therefore start on the day this reaches you. Accept my warmest regards.'[10]

The most important of these forward landing grounds was at Gayadah, built in anticipation of an Arab offensive against the Turks, from where further stretches of the Hejaz railway were bombed in July, including a station. However, there were only three BE2Cs at Gayadah when the rainy season set in. A storm on 16 July damaged all three of them so badly that they had to be taken back to Egypt for refit. At the end of the month, the last machines at

Wehj – led by Ross's successor, Stent – rejoined No. 14 Squadron at Kilo 143 in Palestine, where they were needed for Allenby's new offensive. But both squadrons still had work to do for Lawrence.

Although they knew their planes were making a valuable contribution to the Arab Revolt, the airmen were singularly unenthusiastic about it. For one thing, they disliked 'desert nomads', aware that parties of Bedouin under German officers were fighting for the Turks and that many others were spying. These activities are never mentioned by Lawrence. Wavell, who was on Allenby's Staff, writes that 'The Bedouin … of Sinai were concerned merely to extract profit to themselves, by service as guides or as spies to the nearest, or best, paymaster, or by entirely impartial looting.'[11] This is somewhat different from the picture of them given in Lawrence's *Seven Pillars of Wisdom*.

The legendary Bedouin hospitality was not shown to aircrew who fell into their hands. Stripping Lieutenant Kingsley's clothes off him has already been mentioned, and if they sometimes rescued British airmen who crashed in the Sinai, instead of handing them over to the Turks, they demanded 50 gold sovereigns per head. (The Turks only paid £5.) My father told me how a pilot and observer who made a forced landing found themselves pegged out naked on the sand by Bedouin tribesmen so they could be castrated and tortured to death by the women – the fate so dreaded by Kipling's wounded soldiers in Afghanistan. The pair were rescued just in time by a troop of Turkish cavalry, who galloped up over the dunes from nowhere, sabring the entire encampment.

One of Stuart Reid's paintings in the Imperial War Museum, *The Bott Incident*, shows a crashed scout plane lying upside down in a rocky landscape. Bedouin armed with rifles are standing by the wreckage, one of whom is bending over the helpless pilot with a long knife, while Turkish soldiers run up to save his life. Reid knew how dangerous Bedouin could be in such circumstances. In his account of the incident, Captain Bott (shot down by a Rumpler in the hills near Nablus in April 1918) described 'an unkempt group, with ragged robes and dirty head-dresses and straggling beards and unfriendly eyes – the sort of nomads who, during the lawless days of war, would – and did – cheerfully kill travellers for the sake of a pair of boots, a dress, or a rifle'. He realized 'They were debating some rather debatable points, namely – whether somebody should be killed and stripped, or merely stripped, or whether it would be more worth while to hand him over alive to the Turks.'[12] Interestingly, the Ottoman soldiers who rescued him were not Turks but Syrian Arabs.

My father drew a sharp distinction between Bedouin and other Arabs. He told me that he simply could not understand Lawrence's liking for them. While his reading of the Koran gave him a deep respect for Islam, he found it hard to believe that the 'Bedu' whom he encountered, men very different from the Emir Feisal's tribesmen, had a religion of any sort; so far as he could make out, they did not pray, wash or fast – if there was no water, plenty of sand was available. He may have met the wrong sort of Bedouin, but it shows the impression they made on him.

Everyone in No. 14 Squadron fully accepted Liddell Hart's picture of 'Lawrence and his Arabs appearing out of the desert like unseen mosquitoes, menacing the enemy's communications and distracting his attention'.[13] However, something about him made them uneasy, even if it did not lessen their admiration for his achievement. Perhaps they thought he was too much of a showman, in those exotic robes of white silk or figured damask, which he wore with a red and gold head rope and a jewelled dagger.

C. R. M. F. Cruttwell (nowadays best remembered for a ludicrous feud with Evelyn Waugh), who may have known Lawrence at Oxford in pre-war days, hints at the real reason. In his *History of the Great War*, he writes of him, 'no other figure carried so mysterious a glamour of romance, enhanced ... by his aloofness and wilfulness'.[14] The pilots of No. 14 Squadron sensed that the great man was simply not interested in young British officers: they bored him. He was poor company unless you were the right sort of Bedouin.

Notes

1. Sir A. Wavell, *Allenby*, p. 193.
2. Sir R. Storrs, *Orientations*, p. 246.
3. J. Slater (ed.), *My Warrior Sons*, p. 199.
4. J. Buchan, *Memory Holds the Door*, p. 224.
5. *Ibid.*, p. 225.
6. T. E. Lawrence, *Seven Pillars of Wisdom*, p. 118.
7. W. Raleigh and H. A. Jones, *The War in the Air*, Vol. V, p. 220.
8. *Ibid.*, Vol. V, p. 221.
9. 'Operations Record Book, No. 14 (Bombing) Squadron', p. 20.
10. Raleigh and Jones, *War in the Air*, Vol. V, p. 223n.
11. Colonel A. P. Wavell, *The Palestine Campaigns*, p. 13.
12. A. Bott, *Eastern Nights and Eastern Flights*, pp. 11–12.
13. Sir Basil Liddell Hart, *A History of the World War 1914–18*, pp. 485–6.
14. C. R. M. F. Cruttwell, *A History of the Great War 1914–1918*, p. 613.

CHAPTER 7

THE FIRST BATTLE OF GAZA

**Is it a morbid sense of fun
that makes them send us day by day
a target for the sportive Hun? –
who knows our ways.**

Jeffery Day, 'Dawn'

Now that the Sinai Desert had been cleared of hostile forces and the threat to the Suez Canal was over, it may have seemed there could be little point in invading Turkish territory, with no great strategic gain. Yet London decided that knocking the Ottoman Empire out of the war would be a big boost for Allied morale. If it meant deflecting resources from the Western Front, it would also be a drain on the Central Powers.

Apart from the Staff at GHQ – sardonically described by one historian as inhabiting the 'Capuan splendours of remote Cairo' – both officers and men felt that everything had ground to a halt. We know, of course, with hindsight that General Murray was preparing an offensive. However, he did so with such secrecy and wearisome attention to detail that a demoralizing boredom spread all over the entire front.

The March 1917 issue of *The Gnome*, with its optimistic assessment, was clearly intended as an attempt to cheer up a despondent RFC.

> 'All's Well' is the verdict on reviewing the war as a whole since we last went to press. The enemy has been constantly and badly heckled on the main battle-front in the west and appears to stand indifferently well. On the Italian front in the grip of the weather everything has been held steady and immovable. [This was written well before the Italians' disaster at Caporetto.] The Germans have had some considerable measure of success in Roumania, but their success carries no ease to their embarrassment, which would be almost comedy if it were not for the horrific tragedy of the business. From the Caucasus there is little or no news. On the Tigris and in Syria the Turks have been harassed

and compelled to retire appreciably. From Macedonia since the brilliant capture of Monastir, nothing remarkable has been reported. Germany has put forward some suggestions anent peace. This was answered soberly and firmly by the Entente, which reply induced the Kaiser to address an order to his army and navy composed in the best 'mailed fist' style.

The editor of *The Gnome* then took a swipe at Wilhelm II.

When we read these orders of the Kaiser we are seriously convinced that his is a mentality which can only be satisfied in the lunatic asylum. There he could be harmlessly the great war-lord, the arbiter of the world, the 'mailed-fist' of the ages. We have in such institutions seen similar exalted personages, happy and harmless. It would be sad to see the once Emperor of Germany busy drilling dozens of indiarubber skittles and pacing the exercise ground with a wooden sword, but it is far, far sadder to see him playing the devil with hosts of fine peoples.[1]

The invasion of Palestine depended on whether 'Easterners' were in the ascendant in London – men who believed the Central Powers were most vulnerable in the east and that Turkey was their weakest member. But Easterners did not necessarily see Palestine as the crucial sector. If the Allies' repulse at Gallipoli had momentarily made the 'sideshow' in Palestine seem more important, there was the other sideshow of the Salonika Front, against the Austrians and Bulgarians, which increasingly diverted troops and supplies. In any case, the needs of the Western Front always took precedence.

Even so, since early 1917 Murray had been urged to attack the Turks in Palestine and help the spring offensives elsewhere. It needed pressure to make him move because – always the staff officer – he believed that huge resources in men and munitions were needed, and that daunting problems of water and transport must first be overcome. No doubt he was a fine administrator who made possible the victories of his successor. Yet it was not so much shortages as his sheer lack of aggression that delayed an offensive against a Turkish army inferior in numbers and weaponry.

In the meantime, 5th Wing continued flying, which meant the usual routine of watching out for enemy troop movements, photographing and bombing. The principal targets were the German aerodrome at Ramleh, together with Junction Station – a key link in Turkish communications – and various points along the railway north of the Wadi el Hesi. On one of these raids, on 20 March, Lieutenant McNamara of No. 1 Squadron (a schoolmaster from Waranga, Victoria, in civilian life) won the first Victoria Cross to be awarded to a flying officer in the Middle East. Here is the record from the Squadron's war diary:

> During March on the railway near Tell el Hesi, Captain Rutherford of No. 1 (Australian) Squadron, on a BE2C, was forced to land with engine trouble. Lieutenant McNamara, on a Martinsyde Scout, descended under heavy fire to his rescue, in spite of the fact that he had already been severely wounded in the thigh. He landed about 200 yards from the BE2C, but owing to his wound was unable to get out of the machine.
>
> Captain Rutherford ran to ask his assistance to re-start his engine. As this was not possible and as hostile cavalry were approaching it was decided to leave at once in the Martinsyde. Captain Rutherford climbed on the fuselage behind Lieutenant McNamara, but in taking off, the latter, owing to his injured leg, was unable to keep the machine straight and it turned over. The two officers extricated themselves and set the machine on fire. Meanwhile the pilots of two other aeroplanes, realizing the situation, attacked and held off the cavalry by repeatedly sweeping them with bursts of machine-gun fire.
>
> Captain Rutherford then assisted Lieutenant McNamara to the BE2C and lifted him into the pilot's seat. Then, still under heavy fire, he swung the propeller and climbed into the observer's seat. Lieutenant McNamara took off successfully and although weak from loss of blood, managed to fly the BE2C back to his aerodrome, a distance of seventy miles.[2]

When the Sappers had completed the railway from Ismailia to Rafa, Murray at last felt ready to mount his onslaught on Turkish Palestine in what he thought was such overwhelming strength that the Turks would be incapable of resisting. He intended to advance along the coast, so that the pipeline from Qantara could bring sufficient water for his men. His first objective was the ancient city of Gaza, which stood on a low hill near the Mediterranean shore. Although the front line was no longer in the Sinai, much of the surrounding landscape was a bleak wilderness without water. Beyond the corn land around the city's gardens, olive groves and palm trees, there were wide stretches of rock, desert or scrub, while 3 miles of sand dunes lay between it and the sea.

At this date the place was still only a strongly held outpost rather than a strongpoint, and its capture did not seem to present too much difficulty.

Map 2. Southern Palestine

Murray gave Lieutenant-General Sir Charles Dobell the task of taking it, telling him to start his offensive on 26 March. A Desert Column of cavalry and cameliers under Lieutenant-General Sir Philip Chetwode was to launch a swift attack and establish a cavalry screen east of the town, so as to block any attempt by the enemy to send in reinforcements. At the same time, the main body of infantry would smash its way in from the south, with Australian and New Zealand horse attacking from the coast.

On 24 March Dobell issued orders to 5th Wing. A permanent contact patrol of one aeroplane was to fly over the Desert Column, reporting direct to Chetwode's battle headquarters, which would forward any information to Dobell's headquarters. In addition, five aircraft were detailed for general reconnaissance, reporting to Dobell; any information they obtained was to be dropped on the headquarters of both Chetwode and Dobell. A further six planes were detailed for cooperation with the artillery, which had 'wireless-receiving stations' (Morse-code machines). And six more were given patrol duties.

A supplementary order was issued next day:

> If during the attack on Gaza the enemy should make any forward movement in strength from the Tell en Nejile–Huj area or the Tell esh Sheria–Abu Hureira area, or from both, the O.C. 5th Wing, Royal Flying Corps, will prepare immediate arrangements for sending out all available offensive machines for offensive action against the advancing enemy troops, at the same time reporting his action to Battle Headquarters, Eastern Force.

At the same time, it was made clear that the duties laid down on 24 March were to remain a priority until a specific order was given for offensive action by the RFC.[3]

Biffy Borton had by now taken over from Joubert as commander of 5th Wing, which still consisted of only No. 14 Squadron and the Australian No. 1 Squadron. In view of his aeroplanes' short range, he ordered pilots to operate from a makeshift aerodrome at Rafa, closer to the front line, but to go back to Kilo 143 each night – because of inadequate supplies at Rafa. We know the combined strength of the two squadrons from a return made on 22 March. There were 21 BE2Cs and BE2Es, 14 Martinsydes and 7 Bristol Scouts (excluding the flight with Lawrence). Of these only half could be flown – 12 of the BEs and 9 of the Martinsydes. The figures show the severe toll taken on such flimsy aircraft by the heat, sand and winds of the Sinai, more punishing than all the enemy planes put together.

The war diary records working methods at this time:

> The cavalry during these operations were accompanied by a flying officer from the squadron, who marked out suitable landing grounds on which our machines landed and gave reports of their reconnaissance direct to cavalry headquarters. Wireless personnel were also attached from the squadron to the chief units engaged and wireless messages sent from machines throughout the operations. Messages were also dropped.[4]

The diary adds that planes were also attached to Battle Headquarters. In practice, this meant that six aircraft were detailed for cooperation with the

Considerable organisation was necessary to maintain aircraft and ensure that supplies of indispensable petrol, oil, ammunition and so on arrived regularly. This officer in charge of supplies – Captain A. R. Earle – wears an observer's single wing, but probably spent more time on the ground than in the air. From The Gnome, *August 1917. (Author's collection)*

artillery, six for patrol duties, five for general reconnaissance with the main force and one for permanent contact patrol with the Desert Column. However, should the Turks bring up substantial reinforcements, the Squadron's pilots had orders to abandon these special assignments and join together in attacking the enemy.

Before the battle, it very much looked as if the Turks, who were outnumbered and held their reserves too far back, would not have the slightest chance of withstanding a determined offensive by 28,000 British infantry. Encouragingly, General Murray's intelligence informed him that Gaza was garrisoned by only two battalions. However, it was saved by the Luftstreitkräfte. After the war, Kress von Kressenstein wrote that the reports that German pilots had begun sending in from mid-March warned him a major British assault was coming.[5] As a result, he strengthened the garrison in the city while moving his own command post from Beersheba to Tel el Sheria, so that he would be able to respond quickly. Even so, he had no more than 12,500 men.

When the offensive began at sunrise on 26 March the British advanced across the Wadi Ghazi, 100 yd wide and nearly 50 ft deep, that lay several miles south of Gaza. They did so in a thick fog that did not lift until 7.30 a.m. and took an hour to clear fully. Despite the haze, towards 8.00 a.m. a German pilot

A Halberstadt DII, a German single-seater that arrived in the Sinai shortly before the first Battle of Gaza. 'The Halberstadt fighting pilots, whose aeroplane was speedier and handier than anything flying against them, took every opportunity to attack, and had they been more numerous they might have made it impossible for the Royal Flying Corps to do any useful work', says the official history. Fortunately, Fliegerabteilung 300 possessed only two of them. (Philip Jarrett)

reported that a strong force of British infantry was advancing from the south and that British cavalry and armoured cars had broken through the defences between the city and Tel el Sheria. Kress von Kressenstein immediately gave orders to the German commandant in Gaza, Major Tiller, to hold out to the last man. In addition, he sent troops to attack the British in the rear, but they were too slow and then held up by British cavalry and armoured cars.

As visibility improved, 5th Wing began sending in reports about the battle's progress. The Desert Column had surrounded Gaza by 11.00 a.m. and were followed up by infantry, while some Anzac cavalry actually got inside the city. Henceforward, progress was very slow. Gaza was surrounded by hills and ridges that were covered in cactus hedges with razor-sharp leaves as viciously impenetrable as barbed wire.

Shortly after 4.00 p.m. one of Borton's aircraft flew over the Ali Muntar, a knoll 300 ft high known as 'the watchman' that protected the southern side of the town. The pilot saw that while the infantry (including dismounted cavalry from Chetwode's Desert Column) had taken the Green Hill nearby and overrun a large part of the Ali Muntar, it was being stubbornly defended; even if they overran it, they would have to fight their way through the 'labyrinth', a strongly fortified network of gardens, olive groves and trenches. Graver still, at 4.30 p.m. an aircraft spotted Turkish reinforcements, cavalry and infantry, advancing from Huj. Half an hour later, another plane reported discouragingly that this column – still marching towards Gaza – included about 8,000 infantry.

When the sun set at 6.00 p.m. and darkness fell the British had failed to capture Gaza, while it was known that yet more Turkish reinforcements were on their way. The British commanders did not realize that inside the city Major Tiller was convinced the battle was lost and had blown up his wireless station. In fact Dobell very nearly succeeded. But there had been a disastrous breakdown in communications, his headquarters losing control of the situation.

Dangerously exposed to counter-attack, two major divisions were in the wrong place, while Chetwode's cavalry had become sucked in to the fighting on the Ali Muntar. Both Dobell and Chetwode began to worry about the possibility of a Turkish counter-stroke. There was also a logistic problem that proved decisive. Since there were no proper unloading facilities at Rafa, the nearest railhead, it had always been understood that Gaza must be taken within a day in order to ensure there were adequate water supplies for nearly 30,000 troops.

Accordingly, Chetwode was given permission to withdraw the Desert Column, which meant the end of the entire offensive. The Turks counter-attacked swiftly, recovering all the Ali Muntar together with the Green Hill. In confusion, the British fell back behind the Wadi Ghazi where they had established a new position by 28 March. They had suffered 4,000 casualties, compared to the enemy's 3,000.

Throughout, the planes of 5th Wing had harassed the enemy trenches with bombs and machine-gun fire. During the withdrawal, on 27 March, they tried to bomb the Turkish reinforcements marching towards Gaza. But the enemy moved fast and were safe inside the city by the time the aircraft appeared, so instead they strafed a number of vehicles, camel trains and isolated units still on their way. They also machine-gunned a Turkish column near Sheikh Abbas. In addition, they directed artillery fire from 60-pounder batteries on to stray Turkish units, inflicting heavy casualties.

There were several dogfights, as the aerodromes on both sides were in closer range of each other. Driven down, an enemy two-seater crashed on its own aerodrome at Beersheba on 26 March, while Lieutenant Dell of No. 14 Squadron forced down two German machines over Hareira. Next day, a British aircraft had to make an emergency landing after both pilot and observer had been wounded, one fatally, by fire from an enemy plane. Having seen off two German machines, the pilot of a single-seater from No. 14 Squadron crashed in the sea as a result of engine trouble, but was rescued by cavalry.

Despite possessing a mere handful of aircraft, the Luftstreitkräfte's warnings were the sole reason why Gaza's defences were strengthened and why there was time for the enemy to summon reinforcements. The margin between victory and defeat had been very thin indeed. With air superiority, the British might well have won the First Battle of Gaza. The authors of *War in the Air* are in no doubt why the British did not have such superiority: 'German pilots flew faster and better armed aeroplanes than those with which the Royal Flying Corps was equipped.'[6] Just before the battle they had received eight new two-seater Rumpler C1 aeroplanes, each with a fixed synchronized machine gun firing forward and a rearward-firing flexible-mount gun for the observer, a reconnaissance machine that at this time could outpace any British aircraft.

The Germans had also acquired a couple of Halberstadt DIIs, faster and more manoeuvrable than the Fokker monoplanes, with a better rate of climb. Far superior to any of 5th Wing's scouts, they attacked as often as they could. More of them might have made it impossible for the RFC to leave the ground. As it was, during the battle three British pilots never returned, one being mortally wounded in a dogfight, while three others were wounded but got home.

Fortunately, for the time being the Germans possessed only two of these formidable machines. The Halberstadt, write the authors of *War in the Air*, 'demonstrated on the Sinai–Palestine Front what had been made clear in air-fighting in France, that numbers and courage may never fully compensate, in the air, for inferiority of equipment.'[7] Mercifully, Felmy and his merry men never received any of the Fokker triplanes with which Richthofen and his Jasta would wreak such havoc in France. As it was, between May and July they claimed nine victories.

The knowledge that London would not supply pilots on the Palestine Front with up-to-date aircraft and was putting their lives at risk caused some bitterness in the Squadron. Occasionally, the delivery of an advanced machine showed them what they were missing, such as a solitary Nieuport Bébé which my father was lucky enough to fly once or twice and described as 'a lovely little thing'. (After all, it was French!) No bigger than a Bristol Scout, armed with only a single Lewis gun, this tiny 'Biplan de Chasse' or 'destroyer' is sometimes called the first fighter aircraft. It had put an end to the Fokker scourge in France, where it became the favourite machine of the legendary ace Albert Ball.

During the build-up to the battle, Seward had missed a wonderful opportunity of altering the outcome. Flying back from a solitary bombing raid, he suddenly saw a group of mounted enemy officers below him amid the sand dunes and, swooping down, realized that it was Kress von Kressenstein, with the entire German Staff. Unluckily, his Lewis gun had jammed, while he had used up all his bombs. He told me how bitterly he regretted not being able to kill the lot with a single burst of machine-gun fire.

Notes

1. *The Gnome*, March 1917, p. 3.
2. 'Operations Record Book of No. 1 Squadron, AFC', quoted in W. Raleigh and H. A. Jones, *The War in the Air*, Vol. V, pp. 206–7.
3. Raleigh and Jones, *The War in the Air*, Vol. V, pp. 209–10.
4. 'Operations Record Book, No. 14 (Bombing) Squadron', p. 29.
5. Freiherr F. Kress von Kressenstein, *Zwischen Kaukasus und Sinai: Jahrbuch des Bundes der Asienkämpfer*, Vol. 1, pp. 26–9.
6. Raleigh and Jones, *War in the Air*, Vol. V, p. 214.
7. *Ibid.*, Vol. V, pp. 114–21.

CHAPTER 8

THE 'SEWARD EXPLOIT'

'. . . in the wilderness, to humble thee, and to prove thee.'

Deuteronomy, viii, 2

A very nearly fatal piece of bad luck had prevented Seward from taking a full part in the First Battle of Gaza. What happened to him on 24 March 1917 can be reconstructed from No. 14 Squadron's war diary, from a letter that he sent to his mother three days later – when he must still have been fairly dazed – and from a description he wrote for Stuart Reid in 1919. He also gave me a few extra details.

He was at about 8,500 ft above Ramleh (near Jaffa) in a Jumbo Martinsyde, escorting a BE2C photographing the German aerodrome below, when his plane was hit by anti-aircraft fire in several places. A petrol pipe was broken and he was lucky that his fuel tank did not explode. He says in his letter to his mother:

> After a few minutes the engine stopped. There were two courses open to me. One was to land and surrender after burning the machine. The other was to bring down the machine in the sea and make a dash for it. As I can swim well although out of practice, I decided on the latter. I glided to the sea some miles away during which I undid my safety belt and took off my leather flying-coat. I pancaked the machine into the water about 100 yards out near Esdud.

He had come down about 4 miles north of Ashkelon, which is some 17 miles north of Gaza. What he does not say in the letter to his mother is that his head hit the dashboard, knocking him out for a minute or two. Then he recovered consciousness, to find his cockpit filling with water and the plane about to vanish below the waves. The letter continues:

> As luck would have it, there was a Turkish patrol nearby who ran up and started firing at me. [He thought they must have been Kurdish auxiliary cavalry.] I swam out to sea with bullets hitting the water

all round me. When about 250 yards out I decided to take off all my clothes, which I did with the exception of a little chain on which were Aunt Joey's medal and the one the nun gave me, which I tied round my neck. Then I turned on my back and floated out to sea. The Turks then stopped firing at me. I think they must have thought from my struggles when getting my clothes off that I had been hit, because they appeared to take no further notice of me. Fortunately there was no boat in the neighbourhood.

It was 2 p.m. when I got into the sea and I managed to swim down the coast about ¾ mile out for over four hours. Then I became most exhausted owing to the unusual exertion and the cold which was rather bad, and my legs had been rather bruised when my machine went into the sea. I had great difficulty in getting ashore and was nearly drowned while so doing. When ashore I crawled across the beach and hid for about an hour in the sand dunes until it was dark. This was about two miles up the coast from Ascalon. You must remember that as I had taken off all my clothes except for a chain round my neck I was entirely naked.[1]

He lay amid the sand dunes in a stupor, the stuffing having been knocked out of him by the heavy current. When he regained consciousness, it was pitch black. Despite being stark naked and aware that he would have to go through the Turkish lines, instead of surrendering he decided to walk down the coast past the enemy stronghold at Gaza and make for Deir el Belah, which he knew had been reached by friendly cavalry. The account he gave Stuart Reid provides further details:

I crept out of my hiding place and the first thing I saw was the little new moon for the first time, which cheered me greatly. I then started along the edge of the sea and continued walking as fast as I could for about 9 hours, except on two occasions when I had to swim out to sea a little to avoid enemy patrols, and on three occasions when I lay down to let single Bedouins pass. I walked about thirty miles in this way. The cold was awful and my feet became terribly painful as they got all cut and bruised against shells and rocks.[2]

The tiny compass, only half an inch in diameter, that was sewn into the lining of all officers' tunics to help them escape, had gone down with the

Shot down in March 1917, WELS ditched his plane in the sea and (a former Olympic swimmer) swam several miles down the coast before walking 30 miles more across the desert and through the Turkish lines until picked up by New Zealand cavalry. This is a version by Stuart Reid of his painting in the Imperial War Museum, The Seward Exploit. (Author's collection)

plane. (I have its replacement.) Luckily, he simply had to walk southward, keeping the sea to his right. After crossing the mouth of the Wadi Ghazi, he knew that he was in comparative safety from the enemy – if not from the Bedouin. But by now his bare feet were bleeding.

One detail he did not mention to his mother was that during the night he crossed the Turkish lines. While creeping through them, naked, he was frozen with cold and thought of killing a sentry for his greatcoat. In Japan he had learned how to kill a man very quickly with his bare hands, but the

Turk was so muffled up, with thick cloth around his throat that it was going to be a tricky business – the man might scream, alerting his comrades. So Seward staggered on through the darkness. In future, he always flew with a gralloching knife on a lanyard round his neck just in case he found himself in similar circumstances. (I still have the knife.) He continues to his mother:

> Just before dawn, the cold became so intense that I dug a hole in the sand and lay there in a sort of stupor until the sun appeared when I started walking again. Shortly after this, [at] about 6 a.m., I was found by a trooper of the Wellington Mounted Rifles who gave me his great coat and put me on his horse, and brought me into his Brigade. During the last few hours I had been off my head a little and kept seeing men and lights [including 'brass bands playing and a lovely vision of the Kaiser', as he later told me]. To make it worse, I had had nothing to eat or drink since 8 a.m. the previous day.[3]

Yet somehow he had succeeded in getting within a mile of his objective, Deir el Belah, despite his occasional spells of delirium.

He concludes:

> I rested for 24 hours in a Field Ambulance and the next day was brought back by various methods of travel to the Aerodrome amidst Champagne and rejoicing.

The official *History of the War in the Air* (which uses the story as an example of 'the incidental dangers which flying over Palestine entailed') gives a slightly inaccurate account of the episode, saying that he 'had five times to take to the sea to avoid enemy patrols' which in reality he did only twice, and that he walked no more than 13 miles[4] when, as he himself says, he had in fact covered a good 30,[5] along the coast from east of Esdud to Deir el Belah – as can be verified from a map.

What he does not say, but what his comrades in the Squadron all realized, was that he only survived because of the skills he had acquired to compete in the Olympic Games. No more powerful a swimmer can be imagined. As he explained to me, there had been a viciously strong current flowing against him where he crashed into the sea, so powerful that it would have forced most people, however determined, to land and surrender to the Turkish cavalry. Yet he had managed to swim for 6 miles, besides covering 30 more on foot in less than 24 hours, and without drinking water – not bad for someone who had

have thought from my struggles when getting my clothes off that I had been hit, because they appeared to take no further notice of me. Fortunately there was no boat in the neighbourhood.

It was 2 p.m. when I got into the sea and I managed to swim down the coast about ¾ miles out for over **four hours**. Then I became most exhausted owing to the unusual exertion and the cold which was rather bad and my legs had been rather bruised when my machine went into the sea. I had great difficulty in getting ashore and was nearly drowned while so doing. When ashore I crawled across the beach and hid for about an hour in the sand dunes until it was dark. This was about 2 miles up the coast from Ascalon. You must remember that as I had taken off all my clothes except for a chain round my neck I was entirely naked. When it was dark I crept out of my hiding place

Vehicles of a field ambulance unit in the Sinai after one of the three battles of Gaza – all armies still relied on the horse for basic transport. After his 'swim', WELS spent a day being treated in a field ambulance. (Author's collection)

been rejected by the medics as totally unfit to serve with His Majesty's armed forces.

Throughout, he seems to have felt God was going to bring him safely home. I know this was in his mind, because I found lines from Psalm 119 – in his handwriting – on the back of a photograph of himself in a Martinsyde: 'If I take the wings of the morning and dwell in the uttermost parts of the sea: even there shall also thy hand lead me.'

'Everyone is very excited about it', he says about his adventure in the letter to his mother. He himself seems to have been the least excited of anybody. 'He treated the whole thing as a joke only wanted a day or two off, to get some more kit, so as to get back to work again,' commented Biffy Borton in a letter to his father. 'I said I thought it was the finest show of the war.' Always the good commanding officer, Borton rather spoiled the effect, however, by adding, 'as a matter of fact, I've certainly got two others which rank with it

Left: A page of WELS' letter to his mother of 27 March 1917 describing his adventure – note the RFC writing paper, available at Kilo 143 for officers of No. 14 Squadron. (Author's collection)

and in fact the whole lot of them have been so magnificent, it's invidious to quote instances.'[6]

Borton none the less recommended Seward for a DSO. More immediately, he was sent on leave to Cairo, to recuperate. When he boarded the ferry at Ismailia, he saw there were three generals on board. During the crossing they came up and asked if he knew anything about the RFC officer who had 'done the big swim'. When he said he was the pilot in question, they invited him to dine with them at Shepheard's Hotel. One was Lieutenant-General Sir Philip Chetwode whose Desert Column had recently hit the Turks so hard at Magdhaba and Rafa. (Seward noticed Chetwode's long, amber cigarette holder, an odd sight in the desert.)

At dinner, after questioning Seward about his swim, they told him how they thought the war in Europe was going to develop after the fall of the Tsar, which had happened only a fortnight before. In their view, the Russians would collapse and the Germans would then switch massive reinforcements over from the East to the Western Front and launch an enormous 'push' before the Americans could arrive. They insisted, however, that the great Hun offensive they saw coming was bound to fail. He could not help suspecting there was an element of bravado in their insistence.

The enemy had seen him go down. A communiqué from Constantinople even claimed that on 26 March 'a hostile machine was hit by our anti-aircraft guns and fell in flames'.[7] With their usual impeccable manners the German fliers wrote to say they regretted to inform their British opponents that the crew of the two-seater aircraft that had recently crashed into the sea near Esdud after being shot down had unfortunately drowned. With some satisfaction No. 14 Squadron sent a reply saying that the pilot of 'this single-seater plane' had safely reached home.

Notes

1. WELS, letter to Mrs W. A. Seward of 27 March 1917, WELS Archive.
2. WELS, description for Stuart Reid, *c.* 1919, WELS Archive.
3. WELS, letter to Mrs W. A. Seward.
4. W. Raleigh and H. A. Jones, *The War in the Air*, Vol. V, p. 208.
5. WELS, letter to Mrs W. A. Seward.
6. Lieutenant-Colonel Amyas ('Biffy') Borton, letter of 1 April 1917 to Colonel A. C. Borton, quoted in J. Slater (ed.), *My Warrior Sons*, p. 101.
7. *Kriegs-Chronik Leipziger Neuesten Nachrichten* (courtesy of Hannes Täger).

CHAPTER 9

THE SECOND BATTLE OF GAZA –
STALEMATE

'My breed, the pilots, whose war has been more
chivalrous and clean handed than any other.'

Cecil Lewis, **Sagittarius Rising**

General Murray's report transformed his failure to capture Gaza into near victory. Giving an economical estimate of his own casualties, he multiplied the enemy's losses by three, implying that the Turks had only just escaped annihilation. This masterpiece of misrepresentation was responsible for a fresh disaster. Encouraged by the capture of Baghdad, the Imperial General Staff in London naively expected the revolution in Russia to produce a revitalized Russian Army that would join with the British in crushing the Ottoman Empire in the south-east. They now decided that Murray could smash it in the west as well. On 30 March he received orders to defeat the Turks south of Jerusalem and occupy the Holy City. He was promised all the supplies he would need and the latest weapons – if not the latest aircraft.

His new offensive was doomed from the start. In retrospect, Lawrence called it, 'the last tragedy of Murray, that second attack on Gaza, which London forced on one too weak or too politic to resist ... we went into it, everybody, generals and staff officers, even soldiers, convinced that we should lose'.[1] He could only advance along the coast because of the water problem, and first of all had to take Gaza. Even the General Staff realized that by now the Turks would have turned the entire front into an almost impregnable fortified line, so that a hard, slogging battle like those on the Western Front lay ahead. The weaponry sent out to Palestine as fast as possible included 4,000 gas shells for howitzers, eight Mark 1 heavy tanks (the first ever to be seen in the Middle East) and additional armoured cars.

The Turks were fully prepared even if they only had 18,000 troops. Amid its hills and cactus hedges, Gaza had become a fortress city encased in entrenchments and redoubts, and the strongpoint in a line running eastward

The flashy and overbearing Djemal Pasha, one of the leaders of the 'Young Turks' and Ottoman commander-in-chief in Palestine, where he had a very uneasy relationship with the German advisers who were the Turkish troops' real commanders – his timidity at Second Gaza prevented Kress von Kressenstein from launching a counter-attack and routing the British. After the war he was assassinated by Armenian nationalists for the part he had played in the genocide of their fellow countrymen. (London Library)

from the coast for 12 miles, as far as Hareira – three fortified areas linked by a string of outposts. The 13-mile stretch of road from Hareira to Beersheba was garrisoned by only a single regiment, as they knew the British were unlikely to attack here since no water was available east of Beersheba. Above all, the defenders were commanded by the indomitable Kress von Kressenstein.

Together with No. 14 Squadron's A Flight and the Australian No. 1 Squadron, the headquarters of Biffy Borton's 5th Wing were now at Rafa. Biffy describes it in a letter to his father as 'a delightful spot, near the sea and ... among the sandhills'.[2] Since it was an oasis, adequate supplies of water were available. Advanced Wing headquarters and B Flight were at Deir el Belah.

On 20 April the Wing had a total of 20 BE2Cs and BE2Es, 9 Martinsydes and 2 Bristol Scouts ready to take to the air. (8 BE2Cs, 2 Martinsydes and 7 Bristol Scouts were out of action.) During the build-up for the attack on Gaza their work consisted of reconnaissance and photography: a map of the area, on the scale of 1:40,000, had already been printed from previous photographs.

In their new planes, the Germans frequently tried to disrupt the RFC's reconnaissance activities, but without causing any fatalities – because there were too few of them. Even so, on two occasions they managed to bomb the aerodrome at Rafa without hindrance, killing an officer and two men, besides wounding seven other personnel. Luckily, they failed to damage planes on the ground.

Once again, Sir Charles Dobell was in command. Just as the Turks anticipated, he rejected the idea of trying to turn their flank at Beersheba because of the absence of water outside the town. Outnumbering the defenders two to one and possessing twice as many guns, he opted for a head-on assault, deciding to batter his way into Gaza.

The first stage of the British attack began on 17 April, with a general deployment as troops took up their positions after advancing across the land on the far side of the Wadi Ghazi. Next day, Turkish trenches were shelled unceasingly. On 19 April a tremendous bombardment of the city itself began at dawn, the howitzers firing their gas shells and supported by the heavy guns of the Royal Navy off shore. Then a frontal assault was launched simultaneously by three divisions (instead of one as in the previous month). Dobell's plan was to push headlong through Gaza, after which two of his divisions would establish a strong position to the north and east, while the third division mopped up resistance inside the city.

Although launched with enthusiasm, and despite making some initial gains, the attack stalled fairly soon. Well dug-in, the Turks fought stubbornly. The struggle continued throughout the day, but the British artillery ran out of gas shells, while the primitive tanks proved of little use over such difficult terrain. The enemy's fortifications were simply too strong. When darkness fell, Dobell issued orders for a further attack next day. However, the Turks fought back fiercely during the night, time and again charging out from their trenches and demoralizing their opponents. When dawn came Kress von Kressenstein was preparing a full-scale counter-attack that might have caused havoc, but fortunately for the British he was stopped by the cautious Djemal Pasha.

Early on the morning of 20 April General Dobell realized that his men had suffered enough. His artillery had fallen silent from lack of ammunition, while he was without reserves. He therefore gave orders to disengage immediately, his army falling back into trenches, which they dug well forward of the Wadi Ghazi. Murray had lost the Second Battle of Gaza, irretrievably. British troops had suffered 6,444 casualties compared to Turkish losses of only 2,000.

The authors of *War in the Air* tell us that throughout, despite the haze over Gaza caused by the bombardment, the RFC gave vital information about the progress of the battle. In all, they made 38 flights helping to direct artillery fire. In addition, they strafed a large number of enemy targets, which included 27 batteries.

Their best piece of work came on the morning of 20 April, however, when Dobell had given the order to withdraw. A pilot reported that 2,000 Turkish infantry and 800 cavalry were forming up in a wadi near Hareira, and about to launch a counter-attack on the British right wing. Had this materialized, it might have proved disastrous, but four aircraft from No. 14 Squadron, each carrying a dozen 20-lb bombs, soon dispersed the enemy, inflicting heavy casualties – according to the war diary, they left 'only scattered fleeing remnants'. The pilot who had spotted the abortive attack, Lieutenant W. E. L. Seward, was duly mentioned in dispatches.

5th Wing had suffered some dramatic casualties. On the afternoon of 19 April, watched by thousands of troops, a Martinsyde from No. 14 Squadron attacked a Rumpler but, after making too abrupt a turn, suddenly broke up in mid-air. As it was falling, the doomed pilot could be seen standing up and clinging on to a strut; he was killed instantly when he hit the ground. This may have been Captain Bevan, who, according to the war diary, 'brought down and destroyed an enemy machine and later in the day was himself brought down and killed'.[3]

Nor did the pilots of Fliegerabteilung 300 confine themselves to reconnaissance patrols. 'The enemy, at about this time, made one or two daring raids on our communications', the war diary tells us. 'Adopting our plan in the raids we had made on El Arish when we were still on the western side of Sinai, he proceeded out to sea, turned sharply in over Sinai, landed and blew up parts of our railway and pipe line.'[4] The 'enemy' in this case was a German two-seater piloted by Gerhard Felmy, who came down about 90 miles behind the British lines and laid a charge that blew several feet off the great pipe bringing the water from Qantara to Murray's army – taking home some of the metal as a trophy. However, the pipe was repaired within hours. Such impudence infuriated the British, judging from the war diary: 'In retaliation, squadron machines bombed his aerodrome at Ramleh very heavily, his camps and dumps at Sheria, his reserve camps behind [the] Gaza defences, his railways and stations.'[5]

On 21 April a BE2C from No. 1 Squadron, flown by Lieutenant Steele and escorted by two Martinsydes, flew to bomb Turkish cavalry at Hareira, but was brought down by anti-aircraft fire. Taken prisoner, Steele died of his wounds. Next day, another Australian pilot was forced to land behind Turkish lines after a shell burst beneath his Martinsyde. However, a comrade, Captain Williams, landed to pick him up and brought him safely home. Williams was awarded the DSO. (Later, he commanded No. 1 Squadron.)

A communiqué issued from military headquarters at Constantinople states that during the battle German planes had inflicted heavy losses on the enemy: 'Our pilots showed their superiority in every encounter with the enemy fliers.' It claims that one British aircraft had been shot down by a German pilot, falling in no-man's land, while another had been forced down and its pilot taken prisoner. In addition, 300 kg of bombs had been dropped on enemy camps and supply depots. The communiqué also says that British machines had deliberately bombed the big mosque at Gaza.[6]

This time, even Sir Archibald Murray's imagination failed to produce a report that could conceal his defeat. Sacking General Dobell, while in no way admitting his own inadequacy, he informed his superiors that his army was simply not strong enough for any further offensive in Palestine. The troops settled down to trench warfare north of the Wadi Ghazi. But London still believed that it was possible to defeat the Turks.

Notes

1. T. E. Lawrence, *Seven Pillars of Wisdom*, p. 239.
2. Quoted in J. Slater (ed.), *My Warrior Sons*, p. 112.
3. 'Operations Record Book, No. 14 (Bombing) Squadron', p. 27.
4. *Ibid.*, p. 26.
5. *Ibid.*, p. 26.
6. *Kriegs-Chronik Leipziger Neuesten Nachrichten* (courtesy of Hannes Täger).

CHAPTER *10*

A GENUINE BLIGHTY

**'Death being so near, they tried to make the most of life.
Life often meant for them, *Wein, Weib und Gesang*, and
parties ended with smashed glass, crockery and furniture.'**

Sir Cyril Falls, **The First World War**

S eward was promoted flight commander in May 1917, but what he called
'my swim' had knocked hell out of him, much more than he realized at
the time, and the Second Battle of Gaza had scarcely been therapeutic. He was
starting to show signs of strain. He 'wants a few weeks' leave being shaken
after his experience', wrote the kindly Biffy to his father, Colonel A. C. Borton
at the beginning of June.[1] Leave in Cairo was all very pleasant, but every pilot
dreamed of a genuine 'Blighty' at home.

My father had some idea of the changed atmosphere that he was going to
find in London – notably food rationing – after receiving a letter from 'Frig'
Freeman from his club (not a particularly smart one, although in St James's
Street). Freeman had written asking him to tell everyone at Kilo 143 how
grateful he was for the 'perfectly gorgeous cigarette box' they had given him,
presented by Willock who happened to be on leave at the same time:

> What you must do for me is to thank them all for putting up such a
> damned good show during my last month. Instead of the squadron
> going 'all of a do-da', as any squadron would with me in charge for a
> month, thanks especially to you and Kingsley, but also to Dan, Fluffy,
> Ridhole, the Canadas and the whole bunch of tricks, we outed the
> Australians and did about twice as much work as they did.

Clearly, there was a keen rivalry with their Antipodean comrades. 'Dan' and
'Ridhole' seem to be nicknames for Danby and Riddell, but I cannot identify
'Fluffy' or 'the Canadas'.

'Things ought to be much more bearable now that Allenby has taken over
and I'm sure he'll put up a good show', Freeman wrote. 'Also I bet GHQ won't
remain at the Savoy hotel [in Cairo] for long.' This was a dig at the unloved

General Murray. 'Of course we are working [towards] a strafing squadron but I don't know what sort of machines as yet', he continued. 'Probably SPADS [at that date the latest French scouts] but I don't know for certain. Who should I meet at Malta but poor old [Campbell] Robertson in hospital. However, he is home at last.' This appears to have been the officer who had been so badly burned after lighting a makeshift flare downwind in the dark.

A troopship of the sort on which many RFC officers reached Egypt. This is the one that took WELS to Malta on his way back to England for a 'Blighty' – sent home to rest after what he called 'my swim'. Summer 1917. (Author's collection)

'Blighty is not such a bad place', is how Freeman ended his letter, alluding to the food rationing. 'Very little bread and not many potatoes but OK otherwise. The RFC is becoming enormous and is to be doubled. Everyone in London is RFC and practically all wear c— caps and maternity jackets. However it is a useful method of distinguishing the older from the newer members of the corps as naturally the former do not do so.' Freeman seems to mean that the RFC enjoyed considerable glamour because of the danger it involved, which was why they wore the uniform so ostentatiously, but those who joined became blasé after a few months.[2]

In July Seward left Alexandria for Malta on a transport carrying mules and Egyptian clerical staff. He was the senior military officer on board, although only a (temporary) captain. The Egyptian clerks were outraged when he

ordered them to help muck out the mules' stabling after the mule-keepers fell ill: characteristically, he doubled their duties when a deputation protested. A Sikh risaldar approved, however: 'Sahib, they are dogs and sons of sweepers.' At Malta he boarded another ship, bound for England.

In London he stayed at the long-vanished Cadogan Club at the Eros end of Piccadilly, a hotel rather than a club. From here he sometimes walked to the RFC Club, which was a proper one – after a fashion – in a house in Bruton Street, No. 13, just off Berkeley Square, that was afterwards destroyed during the Blitz. The club was founded in January 1917 and the subscription was 3 guineas a year. It was reasonably comfortable, although the food served in the coffee room was poor, even by the clubland standards of the day – there was little meat on the menu, because of wartime rationing. However, he found the atmosphere there, one of wild high spirits and very hard drinking, a bit too much. He recalled seeing a drunken officer vomiting into the gutter in the street outside. Elsie, the club porter, was holding the man's head and telling him, 'Go on, Sir. Bring it up, Sir. It will do you good, Sir.'[3]

He had his likeness taken by a smart photographer, insisting on being snapped from the side since he had grown morbidly sensitive about his broken nose. (Soon it would suffer much worse damage.) The 'portrait study' gave him an odd, almost Grecian profile. Despite Freeman's reservations, he wore an RFC maternity jacket for the sitting.

Walking down Bond Street one day on his way towards the RFC Club, he happened to see another member of No. 14 Squadron, Captain Baillie, hurrying along on the far side. 'Morning, Baillie, I didn't know you had a Blighty', he shouted across the road. In reply, Baillie merely scowled and then seemed to vanish. Seward felt irritated at such boorish manners, although he did not know him very well. However, when he returned to Palestine, he learned that Baillie had never been back to England at all, but had been shot down at exactly the same time he was seen strolling along Bond Street.

Another time, while going down Piccadilly in civilian clothes 'a horrid little flapper rushed up and stuck a white feather in my button-hole' – branding

Left: *WELS on leave in London, August 1917. He has had himself photographed sideways to hide his broken nose. A few weeks later it would be smashed even flatter in another plane crash – a consequence of his self-appointed role as No. 14 Squadron's test pilot for new aircraft when they reached the Sinai and Palestine, as well as testing re-serviced machines to see if they were airworthy.* (Author's collection)

him a trench-dodger. He was incapable of seeing the irony. Early in August he went down to Kent to stay with Biffy Borton's father at his pretty country house near Maidstone, a visit that he always remembered with pleasure. 'He gave us a most interesting account of his experiences when he fell from Air to Sea off Palestine', wrote old Colonel Borton in his diary. 'He says they want more machines and was not complimentary about Sir A Murray.'[4]

The atmosphere in England was not altogether reassuring. People felt far from convinced the war would be won: contrary to expectation, it was dragging on and on. They were shaken by the air raids, first by Zeppelins, then by big Gotha bombers. A friend told him he had seen the King and Queen being booed as they drove through Liverpool – in those days almost the second city in the realm – and that Queen Mary 'looked worried to death'. It was the year when George V changed the royal family's name to 'Windsor' and secretly persuaded Lloyd George to stop a British battleship from sailing to Russia to rescue the Tsar lest it lead to further unpopularity for the monarchy.

Seward did not trust Lloyd George, who had taken over as Prime Minister from Asquith in December 1916. He regarded him as a near kinsman of

A highly misleading account of WELS's 'swim' appeared in the French press during October 1917, which so impressed his cousin Capitaine Maxime de Tilière of the 15e Chasseurs à Cheval (shown here in pre-war uniform) that he wrote a poem called 'The first aviator to fly over Jerusalem'. From a photograph of 1913. (Author's collection)

the Devil. And he felt the same about France's leaders, 'those vulgar old animals'.

If the 'Troubles' were not yet in full swing, he realized that the Irish situation was growing uglier by the day. Having booed the idealists of the 1916 Easter Rising through the streets of Dublin, the sister island's masses had begun to hope for a social revolution: his mother told him that in Wexford the farmers were refusing to pay their rents to her brother, a major in the Sappers. But London's brutal mishandling of the aftermath of the Rising horrified him. Even if he had condemned the Rising as a betrayal of all those Irishmen who were fighting at the front – far more died fighting for Britain during the first two days of the Somme than those who took part in the Rising – he was shocked by its leaders' executions. None the less, he was convinced that German agents must be responsible for much of the increasingly anti-British feeling, while later he suspected that their work was being carried on by 'Russian Bolsheviks'.

Seward was in two minds about the speeches in Parliament of Mr Noel Pemberton Billing, a Royal Naval Air Service officer, who had recently become an MP and was constantly holding forth in the House of Commons on aerial warfare. He agreed with him that to send inadequately trained pilots to the front in BE2Cs and expose them to lethal Fokkers was no better than murder, but he also thought that in many ways Pemberton Billing was a ridiculous figure. He profoundly disagreed with his suggestion that the RFC and the RNAS should be amalgamated in a new air service.

No doubt he had read an odd piece of period humour published in *Punch* in July 1916 – presumably considered very amusing in its day – that was reprinted in *The Gnome*:

> Mr. Pemberton Billing, whose vigorous speeches on the Air menace have caused so much delight and chagrin (according to the political view), is happily named. There is a je ne sais quoi about his Christian name, suggestive of the novel and sensational, and his surname always arouses tender reminiscences. Mr. BILLING has been unusually honoured in having a well known district named after him – a tribute to his forceful oratory – and at Billingsgate today the phrase, 'There's Air' is always associated with his lifework. Mr. BILLING is said to be very fond of winkles which he eats with a gold pin that matches his wrist-watch.[5]

All too soon, it was time to return to the Middle East. Somehow, Seward managed a detour via Paris to see cousins. Here, he was persuaded to tell his family about his adventure, his account being widely misunderstood. Everybody seemed to think he had been the first Allied airman to have flown over Jerusalem. Cousin Maxime de Tilière wrote a truly appalling poem on the subject, dedicated to 'Cher Éric', whom he flatteringly called 'enfant rude et sportif'.[6]

The press became interested, printing articles about a gallant nephew of that well-known society hostess, the Comtesse de Sommyèvre, who had daringly 'swooped over the Holy City'. L'Intransigeant devoted two columns to his 'swim': it describes admiringly how, after being rescued from the Mediterranean, he slept for 24 hours and then, even before opening his eyes, asked for champagne, 'just like a true French aviator'. (The death of Rodin is announced in the same issue of L'Intransigeant, which also reports how Kerensky has fled, leaving Petrograd in flames.)[7] Mercifully, none of these newspapers ever reached No. 14 Squadron. Eating at Maxim's – where despite food rationing he was able to buy a memorable meal with wonderful wine – he was wrily amused when a man at the next table asked him what was happening in Russia, under the impression that his 'maternity jacket' was some sort of Russian uniform.

When Seward got back to Kilo 143, bringing a portfolio of gramophone records for the mess, he was told that he was going to be awarded the Military Cross and not the DSO. However, he was consoled by his friend Stuart Reid promising to paint his adventure. Called The Seward Exploit, eventually the picture would hang in the Imperial War Museum. The first version of the note in the Museum's catalogue explained that 'by his bravery and determination this officer succeeded in preserving the information that he had collected on his flight'.

Notes

1. J. Slater (ed.), My Warrior Sons, p. 110.
2. H. R. Freeman, letter to WELS, 28 June 1917, WELS Archive.
3. For the RFC Club, see H. Probert and M. Gilbert, '128': The Story of the Royal Air Force Club, pp. 11–19.
4. Slater (ed.), My Warrior Sons, p. 117.
5. Punch, July 1917, reprinted in The Gnome, January 1917, p. 13.
6. Comte M. de Tilière, Les heures de la Patrie.
7. L'Intransigeant, 17 November 1917.

CHAPTER 11

ALLENBY TAKES OVER

*'War may compel us to be merciless, but no war
need compel us to be cads.'*

Captain J. E. Dixon-Spain, The Gnome, August 1917

The Cabinet and the Imperial General Staff had at last seen through Murray. Within a few weeks he was told he would be replaced by General Sir Edmund Allenby, who took over command of the Egyptian Expeditionary Force on 27 June 1917.

A huge man without a single white hair, although born only a year after his predecessor, Allenby looked a decade younger. Having joined the 6th Inniskilling Dragoons in 1882, his ability was recognized during the Boer War and in 1910 he became Inspector-General of Cavalry, a post in which he gained a reputation for meticulous efficiency – and also a nickname, the

'The Bull', General Sir Edmund Allenby, the dynamic, gigantic cavalryman who took over from the discredited General Murray in June 1917, capturing Jerusalem six months later and wiping out three Turkish armies simultaneously in autumn 1918 – the most complete victory of the First World War. His bullying and outbursts of rage sometimes reduced his ADCs to nervous wrecks but he certainly got results. Before his inspections, officers were warned 'CBL' – 'Caution, Bull Loose'. (London Library)

A photograph taken by WELS on 30 May 1917. Written on it is 'Country in front of our lines near El Mendur' (just south of Gaza, showing the Wadi Ghazi). This was during the stalemate after Second Gaza when British troops were bogged down in something not unlike the trench warfare on the Western Front. (Author's collection)

'Bull', because of his enormous size and harsh manner. Yet he was surprisingly complex. Not only a keen field naturalist, he was able to read Strabo's account of ancient Palestine in the original Greek without having to use a dictionary – probably beyond the capability of any modern general.

His appointment was unexpected since, when in command of Third Army in France, he was unfairly blamed by Haig, who disliked him, for failing to exploit a breakthrough at Arras in April 1917. However, after General Smuts had turned down the post, London decided that a cavalry soldier such as

Allenby was ideally suited to command the Egyptian Expeditionary Force. In June Lloyd George told him that he wanted Jerusalem 'as a Christmas present for the British nation' and that he was to ask for all the reinforcements he needed.[1]

As soon as he arrived, he decided that movement was the key to winning battles in Palestine: swift manoeuvring and surprise attacks. In a desert, full use could still be made of cavalry – this was the last war when British units were reckoned in 'sabres' – even if 'cameliers' would play an important role, with a few armoured cars and tanks.

Meanwhile, the British were cooped up in the trenches before Gaza. Although there was no mud and the enemy possessed less barbed wire and fired fewer 'whizz-bangs', in some ways the campaign began to resemble that on the Western Front. In addition, the men in the lines suffered abominably from heat (often 110°F), insect plagues and local diseases. Their morale was on the verge of collapse – Lawrence even goes so far as to speak of a 'broken British Army'.[2]

Fighting was more energetic in the sky, as the squadron war diary records:

> The enemy during periods of full moon made regular nightly attacks on our aerodromes. To prevent our machines being destroyed, they were flown each night to selected ground on the open desert, so that only empty aerodromes were bombed – although heavy retaliation was made for these attacks. Finally a concealed aerodrome which long deceived the enemy was chosen at [Deir el] Belah where the hangars were effectively concealed in fig groves and the whole camp secluded under trees, so that, albeit under conditions which did not parallel those described in Scripture, we were living under our own vine and fig trees.[3]

The front line and Gaza itself were patrolled by RFC aircraft twice a day, observers reporting likely targets to the artillery. When a notoriously accurate enemy anti-aircraft gun was knocked out, the observer in the machine responsible, Captain Williams, was so delighted that he persuaded his pilot to dive down and strafe its team (by passing a scribbled note to his cockpit, the only means of communication in the air). Identified as an ammunition dump, the city mosque was shelled – blowing up with a huge explosion.

A consignment of much needed single-seater planes reached 5th Wing in May. Aircraft already out of date on the Western Front, they included Bristol

Scouts, Bristol monoplanes, Martinsydes and DH2 pusher scouts. The new De Havillands were greeted with joy, according to the war diary.

> These machines being faster and more suited for fighting manoeuvres than the two-seater B.E. machines enabled our artillery patrol and reconnaissance machines to do their work with less molestation, and imposed more restraint on the enemy whose faster climbing and speedier machines had given him marked advantages in his game of fighting and running away.[4]

On 8 July the Luftstreitkräfte once again demonstrated its sharp teeth in a combat with No. 1 Squadron. A BE2C on a reconnaissance flight, escorted by Lieutenant Claude Vautin in a BE12 and by Captain Charles Brookes (a British officer attached to the squadron) in a Martinsyde, was attacked by a Rumpler two-seater and by Gerhard Felmy in an Albatros DIII – the even more effective scout that was replacing the Halberstadt. The Rumpler shot down Brookes, sending his plane into a fatal spin until its wings and tail plane fell off. After a lengthy pursuit Felmy shot off the BE12's propeller, forcing it down, and triumphantly hauled Vautin back to his aerodrome at Ramleh as a prisoner. (It was Felmy's third confirmed 'kill'.)

Two days later, Felmy dropped one of his missives on the Australians' aerodrome. It told them Captain Brookes had been buried with full military honours, but that Vautin was safe and well, 'a very kindly man and gentleman'. Enclosing a photograph of himself with his prisoner, he said he had just taken him on a tour of Jerusalem. Also enclosed, were two letters from Vautin, one to his parents and another to a brother officer, Captain Williams, with a message asking for clothes. On the same afternoon Captain Murray-Jones delivered the kit to the German aerodrome at Huj, together with letters from home and a note of thanks from the Squadron. He flew down within 50 ft of the ground to drop them. The Germans stood outside their mess, waving at him, so he flew down again, circling the aerodrome and waving back.[5]

On 13 July two BE2Es from No. 1 Squadron were shot down after an escort of Martinsydes from No. 14 failed to turn up. The pilot and observer of one machine were both killed. Next morning, Felmy appeared over No. 1 Squadron's aerodrome, looping the loop in greeting and dropping yet another missive. It was addressed to all its members, some of whom had been writing to him:

I beg, this letter not to send in a newspaper. Please send the photo X to the parents of Mr Vautin.

All dear sports,

My joy was very tall, to receive your many letters. Tomorrow Vautin comes, to take all the things and all the letters (with 1 photo), which were dropped. He is a such well educated and genteel boy, that we do with pleasure all what is pleasant for him.

But if you write for us, you must write more distinctly, because our English is not so perfectly that we can read all; the most legible writing has firstly your writing machine, and secondly [Captain] Murray Jones. Vautin has me talked very much of him. I hope to fight with this sport more oftener. I thank him for his kind letter. I thank also for the decoration of the Rising Sun from Mr Lex Macnaughton. Perhaps I can see the sun later in Australia. [This was a cap badge from an Australian slouch hat.]

Too my best thanks for the picture of Mr Brown and for the kind letters and many photos of R. F. Bailly.

In order to answer your questions: 1) 2nd Lt Steele is unfortunately dead: he expired 20. 4. 17. soon after his imprisonment, he was shut down by our archies. 2) Mstr. Heathcote is in captivity and well, I think in the same place as mstr. Palmer and Floyer.

Murray Jones is a very courageous man, we have feeled it in flying and when he came to dropp the things for Vautin so down (perhaps 100 feet). I would like to have his address in Australia, to visit him. And a photo of him and the others, but – I beg – a little more bigger the photos, because I could scarcely perceive your sport[s'] eyesights! Ramadan is not practical for a visite at you, one must fast all the day. For souvineir I have exchanged my watch with Vautin and we haved engraved our names. Where can I disperse more an aqueduct? [He had just blown up an aqueduct at Mustabeig.] Hoping our good condition is continuing long time.

With best wishes for all, who has written to us. With sportly respects

Your *G. Felmy*, Obltn.[6]

While one may laugh at the broken English, one can only respect the writer's manners and gallantry. He behaved like this more than once when Australian airmen were captured. No. 1 Squadron drank his health in their mess.

The Deir el Belah aerodrome was near the sea and all ranks were encouraged to swim. WELS is on the left, while the tall officer with a moustache to his right is a 'balloonatic', Captain Tommy Thornton – formerly of the Green Howards. Early autumn 1917. (Author's collection)

'The air service on each side in the war observed a special chivalry', noted Cutlack, who gave the best definition of the peculiar code that the airmen had developed:

> Each individual engagement was a matter of life or death to either opponent; the one showed the other no mercy, and pursued his foe, if necessary, and where possible, to the ground, shooting at him till the end. But where any flying man was taken prisoner, he was treated by his late adversaries with respect and consideration.[7]

In August Felmy was invalided home to Germany suffering from a variety of the local diseases, in particular from malaria. Although he would return, his absence turned out to be a bad omen for the German fliers. On 1 September the Australian Ross Smith, flying a BE2C, was attacked by Leutnant Schmarje in an Albatros DIII which – even if BEs were better armed than previously – was much the more formidable plane of the two. Yet it was Schmarje who went down, with a bullet through his head. This was Ross Smith's first confirmed kill. He would eventually score eleven, becoming the undisputed leading ace on the Palestine Front.

At Gaza the Egyptian Expeditionary Force entered on what No. 14 Squadron's war diary oddly describes as 'a phase of warfare at trench grips'. For the RFC, it was a time of careful preparation for the offensive ahead. The front was systematically investigated from the air, by direct observation and photography, until all pilots and observers were familiar with every feature of the enemy's defence system. There was intensive training in the use of wireless and cooperation with artillery. Observers were sent to artillery units to discuss what the diary called their 'shoots' and learn about the Gunners' technical problems. Since the aerodromes were within easy reach of the sea, officers and men kept fit by swimming in the wonderfully blue Mediterranean, sometimes at midnight under the moon.

When Seward returned in September he found that Allenby had transformed the situation in Palestine, despite having to compete not only with the needs of Flanders, but those of the Salonika Front. As soon as the new commander arrived, he had moved his GHQ from the Savoy Hotel to an encampment of tents and huts at Umm el Kelab ('mother of dogs') on the Palestine border, in the desert just north of Rafa and not far from Deir el Belah, where he slept on a camp-bed and ate bully beef like everybody else. Accompanied by his staff, he then embarked on a gruelling, bone-breaking five-day inspection – by motor car along unmetalled tracks – of every single camp and unit. After this, he went back to Egypt, to see the base establishments in Cairo and Alexandria, all the offices and workshops. Nor did he forget to visit the hospitals.

Immediately after his inspection, he sent a cable to London with his assessment, asking for further divisions and more artillery, as well as three additional RFC squadrons with up-to-date machines. He was reorganizing his ground forces into two infantry corps and one cavalry corps, and wanted a squadron for each corps. He was well aware that aircraft were his eyes, just as they were for the German officers directing the Turks.

The increasingly familiar sight of their gigantic Commander-in-Chief began to restore confidence. 'He went through the hot, dusty camps of his army like a strong, fresh, reviving wind', concluded the Australian official history. 'Troopers who caught only one fleeting glimpse of him felt that here at last was a man with the natural qualities of a great, driving commander ...'[8] To rebuild morale, he used simple expedients such as promising the men beer and making sure they got it, even if only two bottles of pale ale a head. Another was to allow officers working in offices or on leave in Cairo to wear trousers instead of boots and breeches, which were horribly uncomfortable in the heat, but had been insisted on by Murray. He also gave Lawrence all the help he asked for. 'We learned gradually that he meant exactly what he said, and that what General Allenby could do was enough for his very greediest servant,' says Lawrence in Seven Pillars of Wisdom.[9]

Seward admired the way the new commander was always up at the front in a Rolls-Royce staff car, without an air escort – in contrast to Murray sheltering

A stern-faced RFC brass hat in his Rolls-Royce staff car during 1917 – Brigadier-General
Salmond in a rare bad mood. (Author's collection)

nervously inside his armoured train, guarded by planes overhead. Admittedly,
he did not much care for what he heard about the Bull's rages, which turned
members of his staff into nervous wrecks. Wavell admitted that 'Allenby's
sudden explosions of temper, if he found anything wrong, were to be dreaded
almost as much as an enemy bomb.' Yet the bullying produced results.[10]

On Allenby's instructions, Geoffrey Salmond, promoted brigadier-general,
set about a complete restructuring of the RFC in Palestine. Two new squadrons
were raised, the planes being shipped out from England to be flown by officers
recruited and trained in Egypt. These were Nos. 111 and 113, although the
latter did not materialize until February the following year. In October 1917 a
new Palestine Brigade, RFC, was formed under Salmond, replacing Middle East
Brigade. Biffy Borton took 40th (Army) Wing at Deir el Balah with the new
No. 111 Squadron and Australian No. 67 Squadron, while 5th Wing, also at Deir
el Balah, now found itself under Lieutenant-Colonel A. C. Boddam-Whetham.

No. 14 Squadron was re-equipped with 16 'Quirks' or BE2Es. This was
an updated version of Stability Jane, with improved wings. In practice, it
was much the same machine and intensely disliked by those who flew it.

Constantly flying on reconnaissance or artillery spotting, they knew they were at the mercy of the better-equipped Huns.

My father loathed his new CO, a very different figure from Joubert or Borton. The unfortunately named Boddam-Whetham was a nervous, nagging martinet whom he described as 'a pitiful little creature'. Knowing the man was excessively mean, he revenged himself in the evenings by skinning poor Boddam-Whetham alive at poker, which he played rather well. (Although no gambler, he had uncanny luck at both poker and roulette.)

He was ordered to set up a forward landing ground in the desert, to be manned by a handful of ground crew, and stocked with cans of fuel and water as well as food. Besides being used by planes to avoid night raids on their

Photography by WELS of an encampment next to an advanced airstrip that he set up during late summer 1917, shortly before the Third Battle of Gaza. Note the inhospitable country. Sites like this were often used at night by RFC machines in order to avoid night bombing of their aerodromes by the enemy. They also enabled planes to extend their range, besides serving as emergency landing grounds for aircraft damaged in combat. (Author's collection)

Photograph by WELS of a camouflaged canvas hangar at an advanced airstrip – like the tents, fuel, oil and other supplies, hangars like these were brought up on camels under cover of darkness. (Author's collection)

aerodromes, strips like these enabled machines to extend their range: they also provided havens for damaged aircraft limping home. Having found a flat area amid the dunes, he sent Lieutenant Dempsey (the ex-Legionnaire) ahead, with tents and stores on camelback, accompanied by Egyptian labourers. When he flew in that evening, however, he found that only a single tent had been erected amid the sand and scrub, under which Dempsey sat at a table, sipping whisky and soda. There was an almighty outburst of rage and no doubt Dempsey's table was kicked over.

But my father's rages always ended quickly and the two Irishmen sat up drinking for most of the night. Southern Unionists, they talked gloomily about the looming tragedy at home, although the murders had not yet started. This was the time of the Irish Convention, the last chance of avoiding partition. They blamed 'that damned Lloyd George' for the mess as much as they did the 'beastly Shinners', and – in my father's case, at least – were reluctantly prepared to see a parliament at Dublin after the war if it would avoid breaking with Britain. They were no less despondent about the demoralization of the French Army after months of slaughter at Verdun. (This conversation really took place – I remember my father telling me about it.)

Above, both: *The Bristol Monoplane. WELS was unimpressed by it. He flew this particular aircraft more than once since he always tested new planes. Two rare photographs of a little-known machine, of which only 125 were built and none were sent to fight in France.* (Author's collection)

He resumed his job as an unofficial test pilot, trying out not just his own squadron's machines, but those of No. 111 Squadron, which was also based at Deir el Belah. All First World War aircraft could be dangerous to fly, but some were more risky than others. At first sight the two Bristol monoplanes of No. 111 Squadron seemed promising enough, however. The type's 110 hp Le Rhône engine made it unusually fast, with a top speed of 130 mph, while it was armed with a Vickers machine gun firing through the propeller arc. Yet, despite being described as 'the plane of the future' by historians, according to my father its wings came off if you dived it too fast. 'This could be embarrassing,' he joked. 'Remember, we flew without parachutes.' A mere 125 were ordered after it came into production in 1916, the excuse for not producing more being that it landed at 50 mph and needed too long an airstrip. Just a handful saw service, only in Palestine.

The Bristol monoplane was another case of the War Office sending inferior machines to the 'sideshow' in the Middle East. So too was the Vickers FB19, a scout biplane sent out to Palestine but not to France. When it arrived, its poor performance was a further indication of the low priority given by London to the needs of this particular front.

On one occasion my father took up a new type of Martinsyde, which had a more powerful engine and was intended as a long-range escort. If a bit sluggish, it seemed satisfactory enough and he wondered about making it loop the loop, but for some reason did not bother. Walking across the aerodrome a few days later, he suddenly heard a 'loud rending noise' from the sky above him – looking up, he saw the Martinsyde in the process of disintegrating. The pilot fell several thousand feet on to some stones: no single feature of his face was recognizable, while his body was less than three inches thick. Shortly after the accident, a letter arrived from Britain to warn that on no account should any attempt be made to loop this particular type of aircraft.

Despite being welcomed as the RFC's first single-seater with a machine gun firing directly ahead, the DH2 pusher was another aircraft that needed very careful handling – Seward called it 'fiendish'. It tended to go into a lethal spin, or turn on its nose when landing, during which the engine might burst into flames, or break loose and crush the pilot. Since the engine, a 100 hp Gnome Monosoupape, drenched the pilot in oil from top to toe, returning to base in an inflammable state must always have been nerve-racking. In France it had become known as the 'spinning incinerator', while Cecil Lewis called it a death trap.

The DH2 was a single-seat 'pusher' scout, armed with a Lewis gun firing forward, developed to deal with the Fokker menace on the Western Front. Although fairly manoeuvrable, it was tricky to fly and prone to go into a spin, while its engine frequently drenched the pilot in oil and all too often burst into flames when landing. Widely distrusted, it was un-lovingly known as the 'spinning incinerator'. (Philip Jarrett)

Bad as it was, the DH2 gave pilots on the Palestine Front a slightly better chance of intercepting enemy aircraft. Usually these were first spotted by forward artillery batteries, who telephoned the aerodrome. Then the 'bell', a cylinder from an old aero engine, was rung by hitting it with an iron bar and two pilots on duty took off. Knowing that the enemy was much faster, they tried to fly as high as possible before attacking. But they were seldom successful until the arrival of better aircraft at the end of the year.

Allenby also introduced the kite balloons used in France. In the trench-war conditions at Gaza, these were a great help in augmenting aircraft reconnaissance. Two sections of the 21st Balloon Company arrived in August and were attached to 5th Wing at Deir el Balah. Their crews, a man to each balloon, were skilled observers, trained to watch for enemy troop movements; equipped with parachutes, they bailed out at once with their notes if enemy aircraft appeared. Sending men up in balloons has been compared to tethering goats in the jungle as tiger bait, and could be a terrifying ordeal. In France psychiatric casualties outnumbered wounded among those who manned the balloons, a phenomenon seen in no other branch of the armed services. Yet there are comparatively few records of German pilots shooting them down in Palestine, as happened almost every day on the Western Front – the fliers of Fliegerabteilung 300 seem to have been too gentlemanly to enjoy slaughtering poor, defenceless 'balloonatics'.

Those on the Palestine Front were commanded by a Major Victor Beaufort, a hard-drinking companion of my father, who enjoyed his deplorable sense of humour. The stories he told me about Beaufort are unprintable even today, such as the effects of the special chocolates he sent to girls who had rejected his advances. An unbalanced personality – 'mad, but bloody funny' – in later years he became one of Mosley's Black Shirts before ending up in a lunatic asylum. Beaufort's insanity may have been at least partly due to being used as 'tiger bait'.

Notes

1. Sir A. Wavell, *The Campaign in Palestine*, p. 96.
2. T. E. Lawrence, *Seven Pillars of Wisdom*, p. 390.
3. 'Operations Record Book, No. 14 (Bombing) Squadron', p. 28.
4. 'Operations Record Book', pp. 29–30.
5. F. M. Cutlack, 'The Australian Flying Corps', in *Official History of Australia in the War of 1914–1918*, Vol. VIII, p. 72.
6. A facsimile of Felmy's letter is reproduced in Cutlack, 'The Australian Flying Corps', between pp. 72 and 73.
7. Cutlack, 'The Australian Flying Corps', p. xviii.
8. H. S. Gullett, 'The Australian Imperial Force in Sinai and Palestine 1914–18', in *Official History of Australia in the War of 1914–18*, Vol. VII, p. 357.
9. T. E. Lawrence, *Seven Pillars of Wisdom*, p. 330.
10. Sir A. Wavell, *Allenby*, p. 166.

CHAPTER 12

THE CAVALRY OF THE CLOUDS

**'The heavens are their battlefield. They are the cavalry of
the clouds. High above the squalor and the mud ... their
struggles there by day and night are like a Miltonic
conflict between the winged hosts.'**

David Lloyd George

By today's standards, this florid tribute to the airmen of the First World War
by a Celtic prime minister in bardic mood may sound just a bit overblown.
It must certainly have seemed so to the airmen. As this book stresses, far from
being a 'Miltonic conflict', their primary function was routine reconnaissance,
even if they sometimes had to fend off attacks by enemy machines.

The authors of *The War in the Air* make it plain that during this period at
Gaza the RFC's most important job was photography. There were no maps
of southern Palestine, which had to be surveyed from scratch. By the start
of Allenby's offensive all the key areas of Turkish-held territory would have
been photographed, resulting in 20 sheets of map to a scale of 1:20,000: new
photographs were taken at a rate of nearly 900 a month, over 21,000 prints
being developed from the plates during October alone. Every one of the enemy's
trenches and redoubts was included, pinpointing artillery batteries. (However
cleverly camouflaged, these could often be located by an aerial photograph
revealing a well-used path.)

All this work was processed by the 5th Wing's photographic officer, Lieutenant
Hamshaw-Thomas, with a small team of assistants. Yet, although photographing
enemy positions and troop concentrations had become an art, there was a
crippling shortage of chemicals and water, while makeshift darkrooms in
tents or canvas 'aeroplane cases' were unbearably hot. Conditions improved,
however, when the new Palestine Brigade was set up at the end of October,
with specially built huts as work rooms and adequate supplies of chemicals.

RFC cooperation with the artillery also grew more methodical. Returning
from patrol, pilots and observers now sent their reports by wireless (Morse
code, not 'wireless telephony') via transmitters, who then telephoned them

to headquarters so that fire could be accurately directed onto enemy positions without delay. The transmitters were pulled through the desert on sand sleighs drawn by the Royal Horse Artillery, their operators accompanying them on horseback. There was no shortage of shells and the RFC's meticulous work enabled British guns to inflict casualties on the Turks in their trenches that averaged 500 a month throughout the summer.

Unfortunately, aerial photography still depended on those cumbersome flying camera platforms, the veteran BE2C and its slightly modified version, the BE2E. As it was almost impossible to take them as high as 5,000 ft, they always flew in fear of the Halberstadts. They could only operate with a strong scout escort and even then some of them managed to fall victim to Archie fire.

A few faster, more powerful two-seater RE8s with 140 hp Royal Aircraft Factory engines began to replace BEs, although never entirely. In some ways the RE8 was a superior plane, faster, climbing more quickly and better armed. Sitting in front, the pilot had a machine gun with 'interrupter gear' firing forward through the propeller arc, while the observer behind had a wide field of fire to the rear with two guns on a swivel. But the 'Harry Tate' was tricky to fly, sluggish in responding to control and easy prey for a skilful enemy scout. Seward called it 'a perfectly beastly machine', saying that it was a bit like a nervous horse, always apt to stall or jib. It was also prone to go into a spin, while the engine sometimes burst into flames for no apparent reason, especially if the machine up-ended on its nose after landing – which was one of its favourite tricks. Like the DH2, the RE8 soon earned a name for being an incinerator.

My father told me how he watched two friends burn to death in an RE8. It had landed safely enough at the aerodrome and was taxiing across the sand when suddenly its engine exploded with a big bang. Both men threw up their arms as the flames roared up to hit them, then stiffened, 'leaving two horrible black things'. The noise of the explosion drowned their screams. Everybody in the squadron knew that they stood a good chance of dying the same way.

Most of the new scout machines that reached the Palestine Front were outclassed by the Albatros. If sometimes effective against unaccompanied German reconnaissance aircraft, which they forced to operate at a higher altitude, they were of only limited use as escorts because of their very short range. There was, however, an exception.

This was the Bristol Fighter, half a dozen of which arrived in September. A two-seater with a Vickers machine gun fired through the propeller arc, two Lewis guns fired from the rear cockpit – the observer sat behind – and another

RE8s, nicknamed without affection 'Harry Tates', the new, better-armed but very disappointing two-seaters that began to replace BE2Cs in summer 1917. They had a nasty habit of bursting into flames when landing – WELS called them 'flying incinerators'. (Philip Jarrett)

Lewis gun fired from the top wing, it was better than anything possessed by the Germans, with a top speed of 123 mph and able to climb to 15,000 ft in 19 minutes. Flown as a scout plane, using its front guns as its main weapon and its rear guns as a nasty surprise if attacked from behind, the 'Brisfit' was going to blow the Luftstreitkräfte out of the Palestinian skies. The Germans thought it was 'the work of the devil, and to be avoided at costs'.[1] But for the moment too few were available to make much difference.

Besides photography, cooperation with the artillery and daily reconnaissance flights, there were bombing raids, such as that of 23 June on the enemy aerodrome at Ramleh, when 16-lb and 20-lb bombs were dropped. The object was to distract German attention from a major attack by seaplanes of the RNAS (who were using bombs as big as 65 lb) on the marshalling yard at Tul Keram, where a large amount of supplies had been stockpiled. In the event, this attack was successful, wrecking the station together with several warehouses.

The most ambitious raid occurred on the morning of 24 June, by four BE2Es and four Martinsydes, on a Turkish headquarters camp that had been built on the Mount of Olives just outside Jerusalem. Flown as single-seaters because of their unusually heavy load, the BEs dropped two 112-lb and forty-four 16-lb bombs. Only four of the bombs, 16-pounders, hit the headquarters building, but this was considered satisfactory. 'The return journey was exciting', it is recorded in *The War in the Air*, which cannot be accused of exaggeration. What happened demonstrates the unreliability of the machines the RFC had to fly.

When engine failure forced a BE2E to land behind the enemy lines north of Beersheba, as agreed beforehand a second BE2E landed to pick the pilot up, and so did one of the escorting Martinsyde scouts in order to help. While their pilots were trying to restart the crippled plane's engine, hostile Bedouin rode up and opened fire so, after failing to set the plane alight by firing Very lights into the fuselage, the other two aircraft took off again. A few minutes later, engine trouble forced the second BE2E to land, and the Martinsyde again went down to help. However, when it attempted to take off and find help, its undercarriage broke on the rocky ground. Burying their cameras, machine guns and ammunition in the sand, without much hope the three pilots began trudging through the wilderness in the direction of home. Luckily, they ran into a British cavalry patrol during the afternoon.

In the meantime, the other planes had wasted fuel by circling around the machines that had landed until these took off again. The result was that the remaining BE2Es ran out of petrol and were also forced to land in the desert. Two Martinsydes went down, picking up the BE2 pilots, whom they brought home to Deir el Balah to collect more petrol. Although they flew back immediately to the abandoned aircraft, it was too late. Turkish cavalry had found the machines and set them on fire.[2]

So many damaged machines were being abandoned and burned in the desert that *The Gnome* informed its readers that a song had been written called 'Keep the B.E.s Burning' – inspired by Ivor Novello's 'Keep the Home Fires Burning'.[3]

During this period my father did a good deal of what he called 'strafing', which meant shooting up the enemy. He was not happy about having to shoot camels from the air, however. The Turks did not possess enough rolling stock or motorized transport to bring up all their supplies so they were using long caravans of these animals to carry them, especially to bring food and ammunition to the lines east of Gaza. Led by Bedouin, the caravans were easily spotted as they snaked across the desert, offering tempting targets to British aircraft. In their flight, the terror-stricken creatures ran so frenziedly

An unflattering but apparently only too life-like portrait of Brigadier-General Salmond, who is making an important announcement during a conference at Heliopolis about future RFC operations. The officer with bulging eyes to his right is Captain J. E. Dixon-Spain, editor of The Gnome. *From* The Gnome, *March 1917.* (Author's collection)

to avoid the hail of bullets from the sky that often they twisted up their rear legs with their front ones and dislocated them, rolling over and over on the sand in agony.

By autumn 1917, thanks to Allenby, the mood of the RFC – and the troops on the ground – had completely changed. They realized an offensive was imminent, one that they felt they would win under such a commander. This can be glimpsed in the cheerful optimism with which the editor of *The Gnome* gave his round-up of events on other fronts in his editorial for August, even if he could not say much about what was happening in the Sinai.

> Since we last went to Press lots of things have happened. The Russians have put up an offensive and taken umpteen thousand prisoners which looks well in the communiqués. Bethman Holweg (or is it Wegbeth

Holman? I always get tied up with these comic names!) seems to have
been in hot water. The Brethren in France have taken the Messines–
Wytschaete ridge, right away to Gapaard. We were never sure of our
ability to push Brother Hun back until this last item was effected. But
we know this Messines position well, from the ground and from the air.
With that hopeless gentle ascent from the Douve stream, and quadruple
line of trench works from Messines to Wytschaete, and innumerable
switches and fortified points, it seemed the hardest spot to tackle. If
we can push them out of that it's clear proof they can be pushed out of
anywhere, always given the necessary preparations.

Dixon-Spain then goes on to quote from two letters, written by a pair of RFC
pilots. The first came from Salonika:

I suppose you have heard of poor old R's death? He was with us on
a bomb raid when we ran into the whole Hun Bombing Squadron of
double-engined beasts, all out on the same kind of errand as ourselves.
There was a most unholy mix-up. The air was full of slip-stream and
M.G. bullets. Their Archie people got so excited that they continued to
fire into the sticky mass indiscriminately.

Part of the double-engined-would-be-bombers left early, others left
later but very speedily, 'wrong side up with care'.

It was my first air scrap and I felt very uncomfortable when I saw
the Iron Crosses. My chief impression was that all the evil looking
things and their escorts were chiefly interested in me, a rather natural
but most erroneous impression. They weren't. It was very interesting
and highly instructive, when viewed calmly (afterwards, in the mess).

Is it really true that a lady pilot is going to Egypt from the U.S.A.,
and could she be sent to Salonika? She wouldn't lack an escort.

I am at present flying a two-seater tractor [plane] of very familiar
type and speed. I bet you can't guess what it is.

The other letter quoted by Dixon-Spain came from France:

One feels that this is where the whole show is being settled and one is
glad to have taken a part, however small, in it.

The Hun is going about in flocks of 15 and 20 and more. He has
fairly got the wind up, I think. Over the lines the air is so thick with our
machines at every altitude, from 500 feet to 20,000 feet, one really has

to be careful not to run into anybody! Of course they do come across and go for our sausages [balloons] sometimes.[4]

Reading between the discreet lines of *The Gnome*, it is plain the editor has guessed that Allenby is on the point of launching a big new 'push'. To Seward's bitter disappointment, by the time it came he was no longer flying. On 19 September 1917 he was involved in a near-fatal air accident on the aerodrome at Deir el Belah. So far as I can make out, this happened when he was testing a machine, probably a repaired DH2 belonging to No. 111 Squadron, although it may have been a BE2E. He smashed his nose badly for a third time, while his eyes were damaged by his head hitting the dashboard. Unconscious, he had to be pulled out of the wreckage.

His nose now looked as if it had been beaten flat with a hammer. Already sensitive enough about the damage it had suffered, lying in bed the poor man was horrified by the ruin of a face he saw in his shaving mirror and in compensation started to grow a moustache; by his own account, the effect was so appalling that nurses refused to come near him until he shaved it off – on the pretext that it was too red. The medics managed to tidy up his nose a little, but when they offered to rebuild it with the primitive plastic surgery of the day, he refused, no doubt wisely. 'I might have lost the whole damn thing and had to wear a black patch over the hole', he later confided to his wife.

More than his features were spoiled. After over a year of bombing, strafing, hostile aircraft patrols and reconnaissance flights – and of terrifying crashes – his nerves had been irreparably harmed. (Some aircrew went out of their minds after a single bad crash.) I suspect that he had forced himself to go on testing machines. When he emerged from hospital, three successive medical boards, in October, December and February, would declare him unfit for active service and ground him.

The unrelenting strain on RFC pilots is hard to exaggerate. 'We were always at the mercy of the fragility of the machine and the unreliability of the engine', wrote Cecil Lewis in *Sagittarius Rising*. 'One chance bullet from the ground might cut a thin wire, put the machine out of control, and send us, perfectly whole, plunging to a crash we were powerless to prevent.' He writes of living 'hypnotised not so much by the dread of death – for death, like the sun, is a thing you cannot look at steadily for long – as by the menace of the unforeseen'.[5] All too many friends did not return from patrol, all too often there were empty chairs in the mess. When would one's own turn come?

In a book named *No Parachute*, Air Vice-Marshal Arthur Gould Lee recalled the fear among those who flew in France. 'There were few fliers with any experience of air fighting who were not obsessed to some degree, though usually secretly, with the thought of being shot down in flames.'[6] Of Manfred von Richthofen's 'kills', 54 out of 80 ended in this way. It was the same on the Palestine Front. Aircrew could not forget what they had seen happen to so many comrades – even if they were not shot down, a crash-landing after a damaged fuel tank had soaked their clothes in petrol might just as easily result in their roasting alive. These were not fantasies but a fact of life. Nightmares about a 'flamer' or a 'break-up' could keep the bravest of men awake every night, line their faces, make them hollow-eyed. It sent some mad, or broke the nerves of others for good. Often, the effects were not unlike those of shell-shock – airmen became silent and lethargic, or even lost the ability to talk or walk.

Captain Alan Bott described his feelings on going down in the Judaean hills a few months later, after the observer of a Rumpler had sent a clip of Spandau bullets ripping through his fuel tank:

> On looking over the side, I was horrified to see that underneath the tank the fuselage was black and smouldering. Next instant some wicked-looking sparks merged into a little flame that licked across the centre of the fuselage. A thrill of fear that was so intense as to be almost physical went through me as I switched off, banked the bus over to the left as far as the joy-stick would allow, and holding up its nose with the opposite rudder, went down in a vertical side-slip – the only possible chance of getting to earth before the machine really caught fire ... And I shouted blasphemies into the unhearing air.
>
>   I have no hesitation in saying that I was exquisitely afraid ... for of all deaths that of roasting in an aeroplane while waiting for it break up has always seemed to me the least attractive.

Luckily, the dive put out the flames, although the fuselage still smouldered. But by now his tank was completely emptied of petrol and he had to land on a rocky mountainside, desperately trying to pancake on a tiny patch of grass:

> All I remember is a jarring shock, an uncontrolled dive forward against which instinct protested in vain, an awful sick feeling that lasted for a couple of seconds, and the beginnings of what would have been a colossal headache if unconsciousness had not brought relief ...[7]

A rare example of a motorized ambulance, used on aerodromes where crashes were all too frequent because of the fragility of aircraft. Deir el Belah, autumn 1917. (Author's collection)

In *The Gnome*, Captain Dixon-Spain did his best to help his readership cope with terror by quoting the opinion of that popular author H. G. Wells: 'Everyone feels fear, and your true aristocrat is not one who has eliminated, but one who controls or ignores it.'[8] Which was easier said than done. The very fact that Dixon-Spain mentions it shows how much fear there was in every pilot's mind. Like many of his brother officers, my father always flew with a pistol so that if things went wrong he could 'get it over quickly' – I know he carried one, because he told me that he lost his big Colt automatic when his plane went down in the sea.

Yet the war was far from over for Seward. He still had a lot to contribute to the campaigns ahead, if from behind the front line. And, since he was not far away, his friends in No. 14 Squadron were able to keep him up to date with news of the fighting.

Notes

1. A. Bott, *Eastern Nights and Flights*, p. 5.
2. W. Raleigh and H. A. Jones, *The War in the Air*, Vol. V, pp. 232–3.
3. *The Gnome*, January 1917, p. 13.
4. *Ibid.*, August 1917, pp. 1–2.
5. C. Lewis, *Sagittarius Rising*, pp. 59–60.
6. A. G. Lee, *No Parachute*.
7. Bott, *Eastern Nights*, pp. 8–9. After some months in barbarous Turkish gaols, at Aleppo and Afyon, Bott got himself transferred to a prison in Constantinople by pretending he needed treatment for insanity – and then escaped in the ballast tank of a Russian cargo boat, reaching Salonika by way of Odessa and Varna.
8. *The Gnome*, March 1917, p. 18.

CHAPTER 13

THE THIRD BATTLE OF GAZA

Don't prosper the aerial work
Of German, Austrian or Turk;
But give the impious fellows fits,
And smash them into little bits.

Sir Charles Strachey, 'A Revised Version'
(of 'A Hymn for Airmen' by M. C. D. H.)

Early in October 1917 General Allenby was informed that London wished him to knock Turkey out of the war immediately, with a single offensive. Lloyd George still wanted Jerusalem as a Christmas present. The EEF by now had a ration strength of 200,000 men (if a large percentage were not combat troops), while Allenby's predecessor had provided the infrastructure. What made Allenby's army so unusual in the twentieth century was its high proportion of cavalry – yeomanry regiments, Australian Light Horse, New Zealand Light Horse and Indian lancers. At the same time, it had a small 'Palestine Tank Detachment', together with a number of armoured cars.

The plan was drawn up by General Chetwode. Stressing that the enemy expected another head-on attack on Gaza, he argued that at best an offensive of this sort could only make very minor gains, besides allowing the Turks to regroup. Instead, the enemy's attention should be kept firmly fixed on the city, while the Desert Mounted Corps captured Beersheba – the wells there would provide water for British troops, who could then strike north-west at Turkish communications. After this, an assault on Gaza should stand a much better chance.[1]

Right: *Lieutenant-Colonel (later Major-General) P. C. Groves, a regular – formerly of the King's Shropshire Light Infantry – who was Geoffrey Salmond's chief staff officer (GSO 1) and his right arm throughout the Palestine campaign, and for a time in Macedonia as well. After the war he criticised Air Marshal Trenchard for sending hundreds of 'untrained lads' into action on the Western Front where, because of lack of flying skills, they were shot down in droves. (WELS thought Trenchard was a 'murderer'.) From* The Gnome, *May 1917.* (Author's collection)

An intelligence officer with strong nerves rode into no-man's land, deliberately attracting the attention of Turkish cavalry, who fired at him when he galloped to safety. In his flight he dropped a dispatch case stained with horse's blood: inside it were personal documents and what appeared to be plans for a frontal assault on Gaza. The 'Haversack Ruse' totally deceived the enemy, even Kress von Kressenstein.

Allenby gave orders for Beersheba to be attacked on 31 October. A holding action before Gaza with a big bombardment would confuse the enemy, while Chetwode's XX Corps and Chauvel's Desert Mounted Corps struck at them from the east. The British had nine times as many cavalry as the Turks, twice as many infantry and three guns for every two Turkish guns. Troops moved up into position under cover of darkness.

The RFC's job was to ensure secrecy by preventing air reconnaissance by the enemy. Fortunately, the Luftstreitkräfte was in a parlous condition. We know from a captured report of 29 September, written by Kress von Kressenstein himself, that at that date it possessed just one pair of two-seater-aircraft and two scouts fit for action. Many pilots had been struck down by local diseases, while essential supplies were not reaching the aerodromes. He ruefully noted the numerical superiority of British aircraft, which he estimated at between 30 and 40, and also that their new machines were better than the German scouts. In short, 'The mastery of the air has for some weeks completely passed … to the English.'[2]

Even so, on the day before the attack, the build-up near Beersheba was spotted by a German plane that used the cloudy weather to elude the patrolling British scouts and take photographs. Flying home, however, it was intercepted by one of the few Bristol Fighters and shot down. The pilot and observer tried to escape on foot with their notes and photographic plates, but were captured. Had they managed to get home, it might have changed the course of the forthcoming battle, making the difference between defeat and victory. The new 40th Wing patrolled the skies until the last moment before the attack, having seven encounters with enemy aircraft from 28 to 31 October.

It was almost a miracle that the Bristol Fighter had been available to catch the enemy reconnaissance aircraft. Archibald Wavell, who was on Allenby's staff and must have been reflecting his views, wrote:

> The authorities at home were apt to be short-sighted in the distribution
> of new aeroplanes. When a new type was produced they usually insisted

on equipping all the squadrons on the Western Front before any of
the new machines were sent East. It took many squadrons to produce
much effect in France, while a single squadron could change the whole
balance of air-power on the Palestine front in a few days.[3]

On 28 October, just before the offensive opened, British headquarters
received some alarming news. The Luftstreitkräfte was expecting four more
squadrons, which on past form would be equipped with Germany's most up-
to-date machines. As the RFC only possessed 72 planes, many of doubtful
quality, it looked as if air superiority might revert to the enemy. Allenby
immediately asked London for two more squadrons – one of two flights of
Bristol Fighters and a flight of the new SE5 scouts, and the other with the
DH4a (the latest bomber). However, he was informed that everything that
could be spared from France was urgently needed on the Italian Front.

The news was only too true. Four more Fliegerabteilung units were scheduled
to reach the Sinai in November, with 40 reconnaissance aircraft, 16 Albatros
DIII scouts, 80 airmen and 800 ground staff. A special 'Jasta' (Jagdstaffel
or hunting squadron) of scouts was to be formed, with the name of 'Pascha
Jasta Felmy' after the hero of Fliegerabteilung 300, who would command the
other four squadrons as well. But before sending out these fresh units, Berlin
waited until it was sure that the chaotic armies of Kerensky's Russia had
collapsed beyond recovery. This delay, just a few weeks, deprived the enemy of
any chance of learning where or when Allenby was planning to strike at Gaza
– their few remaining planes being driven out of the sky – and lost them the
war in Palestine. When the Luftstreitkräfte reinforcements reached the front
after the battle was over, they would make little difference, since they were to
be outclassed by a large number of new and superior British machines.

Meanwhile, the Turks were preparing for Allenby's offensive, converting
Gaza – on paper, at least – into an impregnable fortress city. Although the
enemy was short of barbed wire, the approaches were guarded by line upon
line of trenches, enfiladed by machine-gun nests, while the paths through the
cactus-covered dunes were blocked by sandbags. Strongpoints were dotted all
along the front to Beersheba, a large but well-fortified village on the edge of a
rocky wilderness. In addition, the garrison had received reinforcements.

The best of these were yet to come. Eagerly awaited, they consisted of a new,
élite force, optimistically named 'Yilderim' or 'Thunderbolt', formed of battle-
hardened Turkish troops withdrawn from the Balkans, and spearheaded by a

German Asien Korps – 6,500 hand-picked veterans of the Russian Front, who were equipped with howitzers and flame-throwers. For the war in the Middle East had fired the German people's imagination. Often there were photographs of gallant Turkish allies on the cover of Berlin's *Illustrierte Zeitung*, while in Vienna Leo Fall's tuneful melody, 'Die Rose von Stamboul', was the popular song of the moment. In October 1917 the Kaiser visited Constantinople, calling himself (according to some accounts) 'Hadji Mohammed Guilliamo'.

General Erich von Falkenhayn, former Chief of the German General Staff, who took over from Kress von Kressenstein in autumn 1917 and was Allenby's most formidable opponent. But his Yilderim ('Thunderbolt') offensive, eagerly awaited by the Central Powers, was wrecked by the primitive Ottoman railway system – while his four new squadrons of aircraft arrived too late. From a portrait by Franz Triebsch. (London Library)

In addition, Germany sent General Erich von Falkenhayn, former Chief of the General Staff, to the aid of Turkey. A brilliant commander, despite having over-reached himself in trying to destroy the French at Verdun, when given command of the Romanian Front in 1916 he had knocked Romania out of the war in three months. He firmly believed he would be able to restore the flagging fortunes of the Ottoman Empire. However, this archetypal Prussian junker upset the Turks by treating them as savages, insisting that Yilderim's 65 senior officers must all be Germans – apart from a solitary colonel on his staff, no Turk held a rank higher than major – which scarcely made for smooth cooperation. Mustafa Kemal (the future Ataturk) refused to serve under him.

A Halberstadt DIV with Turkish markings. This is a rare example of a plane from the tiny Ottoman Air Force, whose sole unit in the Sinai and Palestine amounted to only a small flight although described as a squadron – German instructors are supervising them. A Turkish observer captured by No. 14 Squadron and entertained to lunch in the mess later explained to his hosts that he had expected to be tortured at the end of the meal. (Philip Jarrett)

Although Enver Pasha, the real ruler of the Ottoman Empire, wanted Yilderim to strike in Mesopotamia, Falkenhayn insisted that Palestine must have priority. After personally inspecting the front line early in September, he placed Fevshi Pasha's Seventh Army at Beersheba, with orders to attack the British right flank as soon as the offensive opened (an attack that never happened). Gaza itself was to be defended by the Eighth Turkish Army under Kress von Kressenstein. Falkenhayn also decided when he arrived that he would keep in reserve at his GHQ a rapid-response force under his own command – made up of Asien Korps and a 'Yilderim Flying Command'.

Luckily for Allenby, Falkenhayn's staff let him down. Crucially, they failed to take into account the fact that the rail and road systems were even more primitive than in Romania. The Yilderim troops had to be brought down by train from Aleppo where they were assembling, but the pitifully inadequate Ottoman railways made it impossible for them to arrive in time. The crack Asien Korps, intended to spearhead his offensive, was held up at a terminus on the Bosporus until November. So were the new planes.

Moreover, Gaza was far from being as strong as it looked. There was not enough barbed wire, while the defenders' weapons were frequently inadequate. (After the battle, as a souvenir Seward acquired a .300 Martini-Henry cavalry carbine dating from the 1870s – God knows where its owner found the ammunition for it.) Sickness in the latrine-less trenches ensured that over a quarter of the garrison were always in hospital, while there were countless cases of desertion, partly because the Turkish staff simply did not know how to look after their men properly, even failing to feed them adequately. One of Falkenhayn's ADCs, Rittmeister Albrecht Krause, always remembered the damage done to fighting spirit by what he called the 'Bully Beef Raid', when the RFC dropped tins of meat on the trenches. After first taking cover from the 'bombs', the famished Turks settled down happily to eat the contents – and realized they might be better fed if taken prisoner.

Few trained Turkish officers were left by now, since the Ottoman Army had been fighting almost continuously since the start of the First Balkan War in 1912 and it was impossible to replace its casualties. At the same time, the press-ganged rank and file were increasingly inferior, ragged levies without any sense of patriotism. In addition, communication was increasingly bad between the Germans and the Turks, who at all levels resented being ordered about by their allies. The former did not grow any friendlier after an incident in which Turkish troops murdered some Australian prisoners in order to steal the gold fillings from their teeth.

A sustained bombardment of Gaza by British Army howitzers, assisted by the guns of the Royal Navy from the Mediterranean, directed by seaplanes from three carriers, which began on 27 October, convinced Kress von Kressenstein that an assault on the city must be coming. Shrewd though he may have been, he refused to credit the tales of British troop movements on the eastern flank that were constantly being brought in by Bedouin spies, even when these were confirmed by an Indian deserter.

As for the RFC's contribution, the war diary recorded the following:

> From dawn till dusk, squadron machines were constantly in the air, watching enemy movement, conveying information to the guns, reporting active enemy batteries, directing fire on undiscovered and active positions, guiding by general corrections the massed fire of our heavy guns on known or suspected enemy headquarters, reserve billets, [ammunition] dumps, water supply areas, telephone and signal

Photograph taken by WELS on 11 May 1917 during the stalemate that set in after the
Second Battle of Gaza, where Murray had failed yet again. On the back it is described as
'Turkish position S of Sh el Baha'. (Author's collection)

headquarters. Incessant and unflagging fire was maintained by day and night.

Machines that bombed by night watched for the flash of enemy guns that had remained silent by day, reporting their position and activity to [their own] gunners.[4]

One reason why planes were able to give the artillery such invaluable help was that there were 53 wireless stations with the specific task of receiving and passing on their reports.

Unfortunately for the Turks, after the British offensive had begun in earnest General von Falkenhayn was absent from the Palestine Front, together with his entire staff. They were kicking their heels on board a train that was miles away, on the miserable single-track railway from Aleppo. As for the pick of the Gaza garrison's eagerly awaited reinforcements, the men of 'Yilderim Flying Command' were still in cattle trucks steaming towards Gaza at the snail's pace that was all the primitive locomotives could manage, while Asien Korps had not even been allocated transport.

If intended as a deception, the bombardment of Gaza caused havoc, demolishing whole areas of the city. Many Turkish batteries inside the perimeter were put out of action: RFC air photography had provided their own gunners with a list of 131, including details of their artillery's calibre – 23 out of 29 batteries having been identified in the city alone. Balloons directed fire from two big guns on to the Turkish station at Beit Hanun 9 miles away, which was where the enemy were expecting the bulk of their reinforcements to disembark.

In the words of Archibald Wavell who took part, 'The operation consisted of a crescendo of blows operating at either end of the Turkish line over twenty miles apart.' He added that the Third Battle of Gaza was a misleading title for what 'should more properly be called the Gaza–Beersheba battle'.[5] At dawn on 31 October British guns began shelling Beersheba, preparing the way for the infantry who went in at 7.45 a.m. A few hours later, seemingly out of the blue, the Desert Mounted Corps (Australians and New Zealanders) attacked from the rocky wasteland east of the city.

Encircled, the Turkish commander of Beersheba sent a frantic appeal for help to Kress von Kressenstein, who refused to send him assistance, unable to believe the situation could be so bad. Just before dusk, with the sunlight in their eyes, the 4th Australian Light Horse charged the remaining Turkish trenches,

The magnificent Australian Light Horse advancing through the Sinai. Fearless and relentlessly pugnacious, during the winter of 1917 they demanded to be equipped with sabres. In contrast to the Western Front, cavalry played a vital role in the Palestine campaign, and the RFC worked closely with them, flying above cavalry charges. (Author's collection)

some troopers dismounting to fight at bayonet point while others, using their bayonets as swords, galloped on into the town to capture the wells before the Turks could destroy them. (As Wavell commented, 'This charge was a gallant affair.') The fall of 'Beersheba of the Seven Wells' turned the enemy's flank.

The RFC played its part to the full, as Biffy Borton recorded:

> For days before the actual attack on Birsheeba [*sic*] we were hard at it – reconnaissance, photography and registering the guns and also trying to make the air as unpleasant as possible to the Hun. We now HAVE FOUR TO OUR CREDIT – 3 within our lines and one in flames just behind their lines, the wreckage having been since seen by our people in their advance.[6]

Not all went smoothly. While General Bulfin continued to hammer the Turkish centre, a contrary wind dispersed his gas attack. (Had it worked, the effect on the Turks would have been horrific – they did not possess a single

A post-war photograph in RAF full dress of Air Vice-Marshal Sir Sefton Brancker, who replaced Salmond in command of the RFC in Palestine from Third Gaza in October 1917 until January 1918. One of the architects of the RAF, he became Director of Civil Aviation, dying in 1930 on the airship R101 when it crashed in flames. (London Library)

gas mask.) At the same time, Allenby's ability to strike at Gaza from the east was hampered by lack of water: the Beersheba wells did not hold as much as expected, so that washing and shaving had to be forbidden. More than one sandstorm blew up, making it impossible to see even a few yards in front. For a day or two the offensive ground to a halt, although Anzac cavalry penetrated a long way behind enemy lines, threatening Jerusalem. Then, stubborn as they were, the Turks began to lose their nerve.

Softening up the enemy for an assault on Gaza from the shore, during the night of 1/2 November, two of No. 14 Squadron's aircraft bombed and machine-gunned their positions by moonlight, knocking out several batteries – located by flashes from their guns. (My father explained that, as there were no luminous dials, pilots had to check their petrol gauges with a torch.) When Turkish infantry were spotted marching down the coast, the pilots informed the artillery, who inflicted heavy casualties.

Early in the offensive (the date has been deleted by the censor) British airmen showed that they could still be just as chivalrous as the pilots of the Luftstreitkräfte. Borton wrote to his father:

I have now taken over what is to be called the 40th Wing R.F.C. I had hoped to stick to my old number [5th Wing] as we had great Esprit de Corps bound up with it. However, we have made a good start by bringing down THE FIRST HUN to come down in our lines on this front. The pilot is a prisoner and is staying here 3 or 4 days with the squadron which brought him down, and the machine is now being repaired and should shortly be flying under our colours. [One of the once-dreaded Halberstadts?] We are all in great glee over it, and hope it will be the first of a series. I enclose a photo of a group of our Pilots and Observers with our captured Hun in the centre, wearing Turkish uniform as he has been attached to the Turk since 1915. He's a good fellow.[7]

During the battle Major-General Sefton Brancker replaced Geoffrey Salmond in command of the RFC in the Middle East. An exuberant, jovial figure with a monocle, he was popularly known as 'Bum-and-Eyeglass' (and as 'Blotto' by close friends from his days in India). Nevertheless, originally a Gunner who had been flying since 1911, despite his colourful appearance he proved to be no less effective than Salmond, working well with Allenby, whom he admired. He was much liked by the Brigade, who enjoyed his ribald sense of humour. Seward met him several times and developed as great a respect for him as he had for Geoffrey Salmond.

Brancker was favourably impressed by the Flying Corps' performance. 'We obtained complete mastery in the air', he writes in a letter of 7 December. 'The German aviator did not show up well on this occasion.'[8] While he did not appreciate the exceptionally difficult conditions under which the Lufstreitskräfte was operating, for the moment it was certainly beginning to look as if the Germans had been shot out of the sky.

Notes

1. Sir A. Wavell, *Allenby*, London, Harrap, 1941, pp. 201–20.
2. F. M. Cutlack, 'The Australian Flying Corps ... 1914–1918', p. 81.
3. Wavell, *Ibid.*, p. 210.
4. 'Operations Record Book, No. 14 (Bombing) Squadron', p. 33.
5. Wavell, *Ibid.*, p. 207.
6. J. Slater (ed.), *My Warrior Sons*, p. 138.
7. Slater, *My Warrior Sons*, p. 127.
8. N. Macmillan, *Sir Sefton Brancker*, p. 173.

CHAPTER *14*

THE CAPTURE OF JERUSALEM

To meet and break and bind
A crazed and driven foe.

Rudyard Kipling, 'For All We Have and Are'

On 2 November a tank attack across the sand dunes smashed the Turkish defences on the coastal sector, while four days later Allenby's troops broke through between Gaza and Beersheba. Next morning his cavalry rode across the smoking, corpse-strewn ruins of what had once been the city of Gaza. On the following day there was a sweeping advance along the entire front. When Falkenhayn finally arrived in Palestine and set up his headquarters at Jerusalem, he ordered Kress von Kressenstein to retreat immediately. The Turkish withdrawal soon turned into a full-scale rout.

In preparation for this, a new B Flight of BE2Cs and BE12s (single-seater versions of the BE2C) had been created as a bombing reserve, ten aircraft whose pilots came from No. 23 Training Squadron in Egypt. 'It was at the third battle of Gaza, with the formation of a special reserve bombing unit, that the offensive idea was given definite expression', write the authors of *The War in the Air*.[1] When the retreat was confirmed on the afternoon of 7 November, not only B Flight but every available machine strafed the fleeing Turks with bombs and machine guns. Next day 18 British two-seaters, escorted by half a dozen scouts, launched two attacks on a new enemy aerodrome at Arak el Menshiye and its adjoining railway station. A total of three enemy planes were destroyed by bombs, while several more were damaged, after which the Germans themselves burned two others as they lacked the men and the petrol to fly them.

Unable to get into the air, after the bombing of Arak el Menshiye, the Luftstreitkräfte withdrew to another airstrip at Et Tine, which was the main ammunition depot and railhead behind the Turkish Eighth Army – and the focal point for enemy trains and transport vehicles – where large numbers of troops had assembled. However, on 9 November the Et Tine aerodrome was hit by 22 bomb-carrying British planes with an escort of scouts, which dropped

128 bombs (mainly 20-pounders but including eight of 100 lb or more). Later, three damaged German aircraft were found, besides a wrecked field gun and plenty of dead Turks. The effect on enemy morale was out of all proportion.

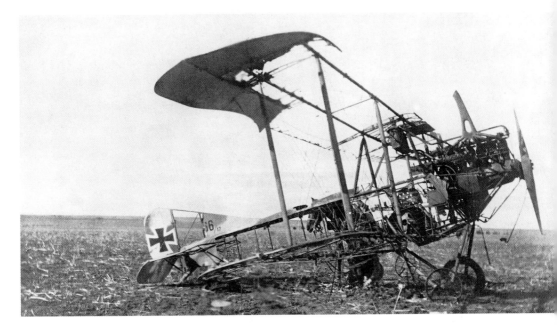

On 8 November 1917, 30 aircraft (nine of them Australian) bombed the enemy railway station and large aerodrome at Arak el Menshiye, setting fire to hangars and destroying eight planes – here is a burned out Rumpler. The Germans hastily evacuated the place. Official photograph. (Author's collection)

Kress von Kressenstein wrote:

> Bombing attacks by unusually big formations of enemy aircraft caused several large explosions in the substantial ammunition dump at Et Tine, which cut all the telegraph cables and telephone lines, creating total chaos. Suddenly news ran like wildfire among our soldiers that British cavalry had broken through the Turks' main line and were approaching Eighth Army headquarters at Et Tine. Although it was just a stupid rumour, quite untrue, it produced so much alarm that a large number of units immediately retreated in defiance of all orders and began running away; many officers and men did not stop until they had reached the safety of Jerusalem or Damascus. Meanwhile, the loss of

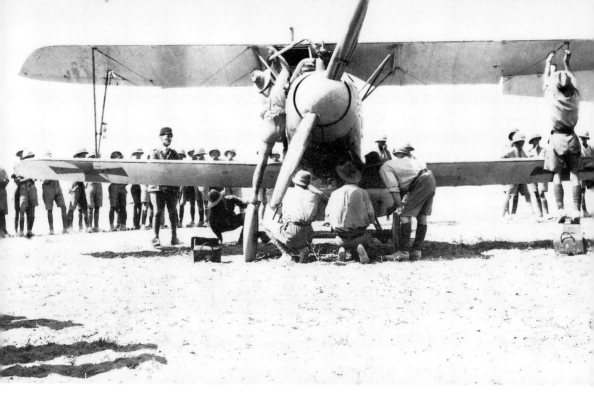

A captured German Albatros, September 1918. Because of the superiority of the Bristol Fighter, at this date German pilots seldom dared to leave the ground. (Author's collection)

contact with front-line troops, as a result of headquarters having been moved about so often during the battle, completely disrupted baggage and supply columns. An especially serious effect of the bombing was that, besides destroying telegraph and telephone links, it stampeded the horses at Army headquarters so that there was absolutely no way of giving orders to the troops.[2]

Quite apart from their being bombed on their makeshift aerodromes, no food, fuel or ammunition could reach the Luftstreitkräfte. The railways were hopelessly disrupted, while the roads were blocked by abandoned lorries, carts and wagons, and the bodies of horses, camels, mules and bullocks – not to mention those of men. There was no means of sending instructions to squadron commanders.

In consequence, the RFC found itself almost unopposed in the air during this period. It launched further successful raids, dropping 700 bombs (mostly 20-pounders) on other targets besides aerodromes between 7 and 14 November. Among the most successful were two on the important strategic position at

Junction Station on 10 and 12 November, directed at rolling stock and troops in the area. A long troop train packed with Turkish reinforcements was shot up at Lydda on 14 November. Moreover, as Brancker pointed out in his letter of 7 December, 'When attacking Junction Station, we destroyed the whole of the telegraphic communication between Jerusalem and the North, thereby forcing the enemy to use wireless, and disclosing to us his plans.'[3] In contrast, throughout Allenby's pursuit unbroken communications between units and his headquarters were maintained by the RFC.[4]

Even BE2Cs were able to get through. Flown without observers in order to carry bigger bombs, on 10 November a pair of these old workhorses were used for a risky attack at low altitude on a key railway bridge over the Wadi es Surar near Junction Station, an area that was swarming with Turkish troops. Each dropped a 112-pounder from just over 500 ft but neither exploded. One of the BE2Cs was brought down by rifle fire only a quarter of a mile away from the bridge, its pilot later dying of his wounds at Damascus as a prisoner of war.

The Turks tried to rally, regrouping shakily 20 miles back. On 8 November Falkenhayn attempted to block the road out of Gaza with a counter-attack at Khuweilfe by Yilderim troops, a small number of whom had at last arrived, but this failed. British and Anzac cavalry kept up the pressure. The enemy started to dig trenches around Junction Station. However, on 14 November it fell to a detachment of armoured cars, securing a steam pumping plant that would provide all the drinking water needed. The Australian Light Horse then beat off a final counter-attack by Falkenhayn, whose men, by now completely marched off their feet, were exhausted as well as outnumbered.

Junction Station's capture and the repulse of Falkenhayn's counter-attack cut the Turks in two. Their Seventh Army withdrew a few miles behind the station, while the remnant of Eighth was still in full retreat. This must have been a nightmare for those caught up in it. In *Greenmantle* John Buchan's evocation of a Turkish rout on another front (Erzerum in the Caucasus) gives us some idea of what took place:

> A crazy, jostling crowd, spreading away beyond the road … the indescribable babbling cries of a beaten army … that maddened horde … men panting and gasping in their flight, many of them bloody from wounds, many tottering in the first stages of collapse and death.[5]

Ramleh, Lydda and Jaffa had all been captured by 16 November. Holding the broken Eighth Army at bay on the coast, Allenby attacked the disintegrating

Seventh in the Judaean Hills, despite its terrain being ideally suited for ambushes. He was determined to deprive Falkenhayn of any chance of regrouping and organizing a defence of Jerusalem.

But the seasonal rains began, which made campaigning in the bleak hills and ravines miserable for cavalry without tents or even blankets. Life was bad enough in the plains, where mud turned the roads into quagmires, while floods destroyed the main railway line. By 20 November, the weather was endangering Allenby's offensive. It was not only bad weather that hampered the RFC, however. Brancker records that 'All our energies were devoted to pushing forward our squadrons close up to our leading troops, a task rendered very difficult by shortage of transport, execrable roads, and the large amount of petrol and oil necessary to keep us running.'[6]

The Turks began to recover, counter-attacking locally. More of Falkenhayn's Yilderim reinforcements reached the front and on 27 November he took advantage of Allenby's momentary shortage of heavy guns to launch a full-scale counter-offensive, which was led by 'Storm Battalions' of picked Turkish soldiers – modelled on the *Stosstruppen* of the Western Front. Despite some fierce fighting, he failed, losing irreplaceable troops.

Turkish prisoners being dispatched from Junction Station in a captured Turkish train, November 1917. The rolling stock is typical of that so frequently bombed by No. 14 Squadron. (Author's collection)

The RFC played a major role throughout this period, beating off counter-offensives and chasing the enemy while they were retreating. By 20 November the whole of No. 14 Squadron found themselves operating from Julis, not far from Ashkelon. Within a week they moved north to the Wadi es Surar near Junction Station, where they stayed for rather longer, although the rest of 5th Wing (No. 113 Squadron) and part of 40th remained at Julis. All squadrons were re-equipped with new machines, RE8s and, for alarm, patrol and escort duty, French Nieuport scouts – excellent Super-Bébé Nieuport 17s of the type flown with such murderous effect by Albert Ball over France. For the moment, there were no more Bristol Fighters. Unmolested, the balloon sections now operated from Saris, not far from Junction Station, or from Lydda. Balloonatics and aircrew alike continued to watch the Turks like vultures, while scouts strafed them without mercy.

The enemy took up new positions in the Judaean sector where the hills, rising from the coastal plain of Palestine, were penetrated by winding passes and by a single, dauntingly steep and narrow main road. Yet, bit by bit, Allenby's infantry forced their way along the road, often at bayonet point. The Turks put up less of a fight than expected. 'Paradoxical as it sounds, Jerusalem was captured at Gaza', comments the war diary. 'The endless bombardment, the whirling uncertainty and nervousness our bombing had induced, had so completely demoralised the Turk that apart from occasional stands he was unable to offer a serious sustained resistance.'[7]

To avoid fighting near the Holy City, an attempt was made to reach the Jerusalem–Nablus road along an old Roman track and isolate it from the north. This advance got as far as Nebi Samweil ridge (from where the city can be seen), but here it was momentarily held up. Heavy guns needed to be manhandled across the hills, the gunners indicating their presence to observers by laying out easily recognizable ground strips. Aircraft marked Turkish targets such as troop concentrations by dropping smoke bombs onto them, the guns firing in the direction of the smoke. During the advance low-flying planes patrolled the road in front of the troops, strafing the least sign of resistance.

Brancker wrote to Salmond early in December:

> The Palestine [RFC] Brigade has done very well in spite of its mixed assortment of machines. Our casualties have been extraordinarily small, even after taking into account the rather poor standard of

German aviation in this part of the world. Through shortage of fighting machines, I am forced to send BE2s considerable distances over the lines without escort and they get on all right, but this cannot last and we shall have trouble soon.

He added that the Luftstreitskräfte was reorganizing and thought that they had about a dozen Albatros DIIIs and perhaps 24 Rumpler two-seaters. These 'will steadily increase as, from Secret Service information, they appear to be bringing up a good many aeroplanes by rail'.[8]

As Brancker had predicted, new German machines had started to reappear towards the end of November, although a large number had been destroyed during a mysterious fire at Aleppo. On the 28th and 29th of the month a new German aerodrome at Tul Keram, north-west of Nablus, which had been quickly identified by the RFC, was bombed twice – by B Flight of No. 14 Squadron and by No. 1 Squadron. Between them, they dropped a hundred 20-pounders on the Germans, but without crippling them. The enemy had acquired several fine airmen, such as Hauptmann Franz Walz, commander of the Bavarian Fliegerabteilung 304, who was nicknamed the 'Eagle of Jericho' on account of some now long-forgotten feat of gallantry. In August 1918 he would be awarded the Pour le Mérite – Imperial Germany's highest decoration – in recognition of his outstanding leadership.

Yet, although its aircraft continued to fly, the Luftstreitkräfte was unable to regain the initiative. During 1918 it would increasingly find itself at a disadvantage as more and more Bristol Fighters arrived. These were joined by an excellent new single-seater scout, the SE5: powered by a 200 hp Wolseley Viper engine, it had a synchronized Vickers gun firing through the propeller and a Lewis gun mounted on the top plane. (Brancker was delighted when, by itself, the first 'Five' to reach Palestine chased off an enemy patrol of four Albatros scouts and two Rumplers.) There were also more Nieuport 17s. Now, it was the British who enjoyed technical superiority in the air.

'It is raining like fury here, and I'm afraid our further advance will be delayed', wrote Brancker on 7 December.[9] None the less, ignoring the unrelenting downpour and the mist, Allenby relaunched his offensive next day, with Jerusalem as his objective. Despite the weather, he insisted the enemy must be bombed and machine-gunned from the air, although the aerodromes had become morasses that made it seemingly impossible for planes to take off. The CO of No. 113 Squadron, Major McCrindle, laid tarpaulins over the glue-

A Nieuport 11 (Bébé), a French scout of which a small number reached the Sinai Front in late summer 1917. WELS called it 'a lovely little thing'. Although better as a fighting machine than anything so far flown by the RFC in Palestine, it was no more than evenly matched against the German 'bull-nosed' Albatros DIII and certainly not its superior.
(Philip Jarrett)

like mud, to make an artificial runway, but only just succeeded in leaving the ground and, after completing a successful reconnaissance mission despite the rain, he found it impossible to return to base; forced to stay in the air, circling, he eventually found a dry patch of sand some miles away on which he made a hazardous landing. Tarpaulins were not the answer.

However, Captain Bates of No. 14 Squadron developed a method of taking off from his water-logged aerodrome that was copied by fellow pilots. After being hauled up to the top of a small hill with ropes which were pulled by teams of navvies from the Egyptian Labour Corps, their planes did a 'flying dive' down the hill that enabled them to get into the air. Despite visibility being almost nil, the squadron managed to fly 50 hours on the rain-sodden 9 December, dropping a hundred 20-pounders on the enemy besides machine-gunning them. On returning from patrol, the machines always became bogged down when they landed and had to be dragged out of the mud by the Egyptian navvies. Even so, 'what reconnaissance work the mist allowed was

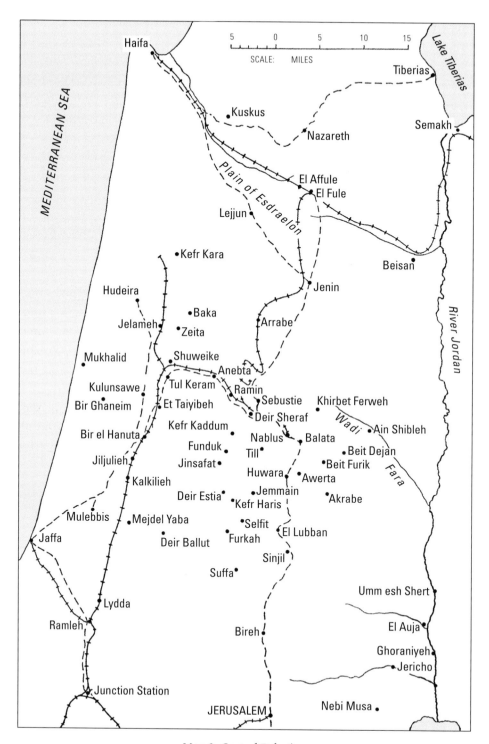

Map 3. Central Palestine

done and No. 14 Squadron had the proud record of being the only squadron in the force which succeeded in defeating the veto of the weather', recorded the war diary.[10]

Although the attack on Jerusalem on 8 December captured the Turks' main defences, when night fell the attackers, blinded by rain and fog, thought that it had stalled. But the enemy had fled, leaving the mayor to surrender. Three days later Allenby entered the Holy City through the Jaffa Gate – on foot, as a sign of humility. (Among the few officers who accompanied him was T. E. Lawrence.) A proclamation was read, promising that the shrines of every faith would be protected. He then went back to his camp.

As promised, the British public had got their Christmas present. In Brancker's words, 'The old Crusaders are avenged.'[11] The loss of Jerusalem was a spectacular humiliation for the Ottoman Empire, particularly after losing Mecca to the Arabs. In celebration, the RFC ordered a Christmas card that was scarcely in the spirit of peace and goodwill: on top was a photograph of the recently captured Holy City – below, a drawing of what appears to be a BE2E shooting down (against all probability) a Fokker *Eindecker*. At home, the news was very welcome after a year that had seen Passchendaele, possibly the most ghastly confrontation of the entire war, during which Britain had suffered 300,000 casualties.

Meanwhile, No. 14 Squadron had been hotly pursuing the enemy, as they retreated to Nablus and then towards Jericho, dropping 100-lb bombs on his marching columns, scoring 20 direct hits – which caused severe casualties. German aircraft still contested the advance, however.

> In the air fighting that took place during these operations one of the squadron pilots was wounded, while in another the observer was so severely wounded that his pilot judged it advisable to land near one of our field hospitals. This he succeeded in doing, but the observer had died before he reached the ground.[12]

'At the end of December the enemy made a determined attempt to recapture Jerusalem, from the north east side', continues the war diary, referring to a ferocious onslaught on the 27th of the month by crack Turkish infantry, who had just reached the front. (Even now, the Asien Korps had not yet arrived, but was still in transit.) 'Squadron machines co-operating with the artillery harassed his advance. Our counter-attack followed, in which our machines bombed and machine-gunned the Turks from low heights.'[13]

Torrential rains brought Allenby's campaign grinding to a halt in the Judaean Hills during winter 1917–18, making it almost impossible for planes on both sides to take off or land. An RFC officer stands outside his tent, trying to make the best of it. (Author's collection)

When the Turkish attack was spent, Allenby's swift counter-attack resulted in a general advance into Mount Ephraim. Bireh and Ramallah were seized and the retreating enemy bombed and scattered. Groups trying to escape east to the Jordan became a terrified rabble under the bombing. Packed with fleeing troops, Jordan Bridge and the area around were particularly heavily strafed, resulting in the destruction of many lorries and wagons.

Then, however, 'The weather in the next two months made further advance hopeless', the diarist tells us. 'Palestine weather at this time of the year is of the wettest. The country is virtually a bog, soaked with the rain which is virtually its only supply for the [entire] year. Machines could not be got off the ground.'[14] Any further advance was confined to the few roads, rudimentary at the best of times and already badly damaged by all the heavy traffic and choked with discarded Turkish equipment. To make matters worse, torrential floods swamped them, besides sweeping away the railway bridges. Food, ammunition and fuel could not be brought up to the front. Instead of continuing the offensive, the troops had to construct new roads and bridges.

> Christmas Eve and [Christmas] Day were among the stormiest in our experience. Most of the camp was blown down though the machines and stores were saved. Still, the Christmas festivity promised [to] the men, which their steady efficiency had surely deserved, was provided. The replacement of our war worn machines by new machines flown direct from Cairo enabled us to provide the wonted fare – by air.[15]

A forward landing ground had been established at Jerusalem, enabling the men to visit it, together with Bethlehem. Meanwhile, a few reconnaissance

The RFC Middle East Brigade Christmas card for 1917. Above, Jerusalem, captured on 9 December; below, a BE2C shoots down a Fokker Eindecker. *(Author's collection)*

patrols were flown when the rain lifted sufficiently for planes to take off, but even if they could get into the air, low mist and cloud generally made observation impossible. One or two bombing expeditions were made on the enemy camps and aerodromes at Jenin or Tul Keram, although only on the rare occasions when weather permitted. The cold and wet were a trial for troops who for two years had been accustomed to the heat of Sinai, yet they remained in good spirits.

Notes

1. W. Raleigh and H. A. Jones, *The War in the Air*, Vol. V, p. 241.
2. F. Freiherr Kress von Kressenstein, *Mit den Turken zum SuezKanal*, Vol. I, p. 51.
3. Brancker quoted in N. Macmillan, *Sir Sefton Brancker*, p. 173.
4. 'Operations Record Book, No. 14 (Bombing) Squadron', p. 34.
5. J. Buchan, *Greenmantle*, p. 6.
6. Brancker quoted in Macmillan, *Sir Sefton Brancker*, p. 174.
7. 'Operations Record Book', p. 33.
8. Brancker quoted in Macmillan, *Sir Sefton Brancker*, p. 177.
9. *Ibid.*, p. 179.
10. 'Operations Record Book', p. 39.
11. Brancker quoted in Macmillan, *Sir Sefton Brancker*, p. 174.
12. 'Operations Record Book', p. 39.
13. *Ibid.*, p. 40.
14. *Ibid.*, p. 40.
15. *Ibid.*, p. 41.

CHAPTER 15

THE SCHOOL OF AERONAUTICS

What man hears aught except the groaning guns?

Rudyard Kipling, 'The Fabulists', 1914–18

In the meantime, Seward had listened eagerly to reports of Third Gaza and the Jerusalem campaign, furious at being unable to take part. Friends from the Squadron gave him the latest news. Since October he had been attached to the School of Aerial Gunnery at Abu Qir, in command of B Flight. A photograph of January 1918 shows him there, standing next to an RE8 with Captain Emmet, the other flight commander.

Withdrawn from front-line service after five major crashes besides being shot down, to his irritation WELS was seconded to the School of Aerial Gunnery at Abu Qir, where he taught 'dogfighting' and strafing troops from the air. Here he is (left) in January 1918, standing next to an RE8 with the other flight commander, Captain Emmet. (Author's collection)

He had not been forbidden to fly, only from flying at the front, and was told that he might be allowed to return to full active service at a future date. On another photograph, dated 25 February 1918, he has written with an indelible pencil, 'Me in a Martinsyde Scout over the Judaean Hills, taken from another aircraft at about 18,000 feet.' (It was the same type of machine in which he had been shot down over Ramleh.) By now this was completely safe country, cleared of any remaining Turkish troops, let alone hostile planes or artillery.

WELS has pencilled on the back, 'Me in a Martinsyde Scout over Judean Hills taken from another aircraft at about 18,000 ft.' Written on top is '25.2.18, country W. of Dead Sea'. By now this was an area well inside British territory. (Author's collection)

On training flights behind the front lines he was constantly struck by the contrast between the Sinai and Palestine with its bleak rocky hills, its patches of green amid the wasteland, its fertile plains and its ancient white towns with wonderful names. He was astonished at the sheer variety of scenery in so small a country. He recalled that, while finding it awesome, he fell in love with it at once. He said he felt in every fibre of his being that this was the Holy Land.

What he taught during the winter of 1917–18 fell roughly into two categories. One of these was 'aerial combat' – basically dogfighting. The other was supporting ground troops, whether infantry or cavalry, by giving them as much assistance from the air as possible – otherwise called 'strafing'.

During the previous spring, he had been given an opportunity of putting into practice what he was going to teach at the School of Aerial Gunnery. On the way back from a reconnaissance patrol in his Martinsyde, he suddenly saw far below him in the desert a squadron of Indian lancers (possibly the Jhodpore Lancers) forming up behind high sand dunes. They were preparing to ambush an unsuspecting squadron of Turkish lancers who were riding past on the other side of the dunes. As he recalled, he dived down and gave them a helping hand:

> When the Indians charged, I flew over them at a height of only about twenty feet, using my Lewis gun to maximum effect, and it really was a *'bonne affaire'*. I made the most awful mess of the poor bloody enemy. There were dead and dying Turks all over the place, with their wretched horses lying in heaps, kicking and screaming, while the rest were bolting in every direction.[1]

He shared the view that the war amounted to a 20th-century crusade, even if this was not what Allenby thought. In my father's opinion the Crusades had been medieval France's greatest achievement and he was proud to think he was fighting in something similar. Although a non-practising Catholic, he remained very much *croyant*, and soon made a personal pilgrimage to Jerusalem. Here, when he was visiting a church, some French nuns pointed out a mark on the pavement that they said was the footprint of Christ. They must have been surprised to see so British-seeming an officer, booted and spurred, hurl himself to the ground and kiss it, just like a pious young Frenchman.

In March 1918 Seward was posted to No. 3 School of Aeronautics at Heliopolis, as an instructor on the staff of the CO, Major Pargiter. The school had originated in August 1916 as a technical training course given by Dixon-Spain and other officers in the ante-room of No. 14 Squadron's mess. By now it was providing pupil pilots and observers with a month's course in navigation,

Indian lancers in Palestine, 1917. When a squadron of this sort charged a squadron of Turkish cavalry (after lying in ambush behind a sand dune) WELS flew above them in his Martinsyde, using his Lewis gun to maximum effect. (Author's collection)

engine management, aeroplane rigging and artillery observation. Numbering over 700, the cadets had to pass an examination (which 50 per cent failed) before going on to a training wing.

By autumn 1918 British planes of what by then had become the largest air service in the world would be in action on six fronts. New types of aircraft, technically superior to those of the enemy, were giving the Allies total superiority in the sky. In consequence, a vast supply of new pilots was needed but, because of the shortage of manpower caused by the casualty rate on the Western Front, officer recruits could no longer be spared from home or Flanders. They had to come from the army in the Middle East, many from 'the rank and file', who were first attached to a cadet wing, although officer pupils could apply to be received direct by the training wing.

There were many observers, including my father, who privately thought this desperate attempt to turn out new officers and gentlemen was 'scraping the bottom of the barrel'. More than a few of those commissioned came from noticeably humble backgrounds – as happened in all services towards the end of the war – receiving the unkind name of 'TGs', which meant 'temporary gentlemen'. (Fifty years ago, I remember seeing an aged, red-coated shoeblack plying his trade in Piccadilly, with a cardboard label round his neck that proudly read, 'Ex-RFC Officer'.)

Only a small proportion of the pupils qualified to wear wings, but even so the system produced several hundred fully trained pilots during 1918. Despite a fair number going to the Western Front, many of them flew Allenby's aircraft. In contrast, the Luftstreitkräfte in Palestine was receiving almost no new aircrew.

'No one who left the desert aerodrome at Heliopolis [in 1916] visualised a day in the later stages of the war when it would be a huge flying town where all the varied activities that war had forced into the purview of our flying forces would be studied and practised', comments the war diary at the end of 1918.[2] Yet the town was pleasant enough, and Seward was delighted to learn that it had grown up around what had been the temple of Jupiter Ammon. The School of Aeronautics occupied the entire Heliopolis Palace Hotel, while he shared a villa in the town with his CO, Major Pargiter. In rather morbid taste, he decorated his rooms with hideous hangings from the Egyptian *Book of the Dead* since he remained fascinated by Egyptology. He was able to keep a handsome black cat, convinced that the animal would bring him luck.

He also acquired Mohammed, a superlative Sudanese servant whose frantic devotion to duty was ascribed to an unlucky visit to the local police station. In a painful case of mistaken identity – he was simply delivering a note – before he could explain, the poor fellow had been immediately up-ended by the Egyptian *bimbashi* in the traditional Turkish way and given the bastinado, after which he was unable to walk for a week. Instead of demanding some sort of compensation for the unfortunate Mohammed, my father found the incident hilarious.

Pargiter seemed oddly reserved. The house was firmly divided into two, with separate dining rooms, no one being allowed to enter the CO's half. One day Seward returned to see him being carried away, strapped to a stretcher and howling his head off. Going into Pargiter's part of the villa, he found every room littered with gin bottles. Yet this was the start of a new career. Years afterwards, listening to a sermon in the Jesuit church at Farm Street in London, my father suddenly thought the preacher's voice sounded familiar and, looking up, saw in the pulpit the Rev Fr Pargiter, SJ.

He became second-in-command of the school, often acting as its CO. I suspect that his pupils found him intolerant of any slowness in understanding, ferocious in dealing with breaches of discipline. He had unexpected problems. The school took Greek cadets after Greece's recent

By the end of the war the RAF in Egypt was training pilots on a massive scale. Here is WELS as second-in-command of No 3 School of Aeronautics at Heliopolis, sitting among its large staff, left of Major Bayley, the CO, both with swagger sticks in the middle of the front row. (Army ranks were still used in the RAF.) October 1918. WELS's face is noticeably thin because he has just recovered from the 'Spanish flu' that killed 300 members of the School. (Author's collection)

entry into the war and sergeant instructors were constantly complaining about their fondness for drenching themselves in scent. More serious was an outbreak of Spanish flu, which within a fortnight killed 300 of his pupil pilots and observers.

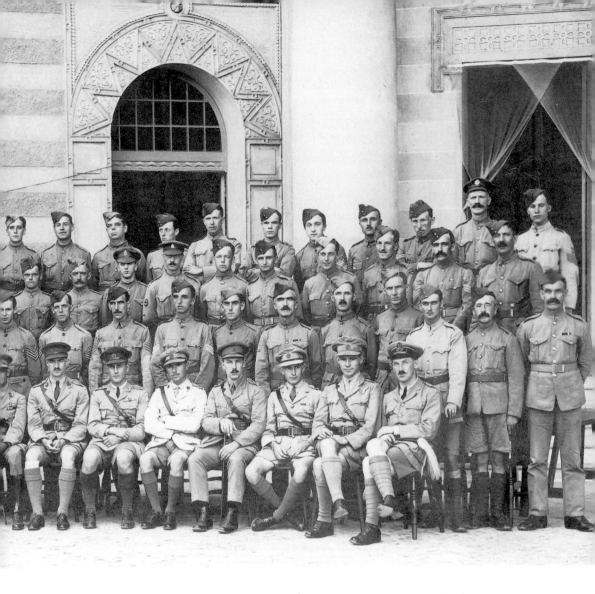

Like many brother officers, he disliked the merger of the RFC with the RNAS in the new Royal Air Force, which took place on 1 April 1918. 'A suitable date', he commented at the time. He was proud of the Corps and had always thought of himself as a soldier. 'Maternity jackets' and forage caps were replaced by a new uniform and insignia, but new ranks were not announced until the autumn of 1919. In the event, senior officers remained the same and the RAF was merely the RFC under a different name.

Although he did not find any kindred spirits among his fellow instructors, let alone among the cadets, he kept in touch with comrades from No. 14 Squadron when they turned up on leave in Cairo, particularly with Stuart Reid, and was always eager to hear news from the front. In fact, he loathed being an instructor and longed to return to active service. He even dreamed of being sent to fight in France.

Despite plenty of hair-raising action in Palestine, many pilots in No. 14 Squadron regretted they were not serving on the Western Front, in the 'really big show', although they would run a far higher chance of being killed. The average life expectancy of an RFC pilot in Flanders, never long, had dropped to two months during 'Bloody April' in 1917. Part of the reason for this appalling casualty rate was the new Albatros DIII, but the main cause, according to my father, was General Trenchard, who sent into action hundreds of young pilots with as little as 17½ hours of flying experience. Lloyd George and Haig were demanding as many planes in action as possible and if Trenchard did not provide them, his career would be at stake. Yet, regardless of the carnage, pilots still wanted to leave the Sinai and fly in France.

Tales filtered through from the main theatre of war that appealed to my father's savage streak. He particularly admired a friend who had led a bayonet charge with an eye half shot out and hanging down on his cheek, and blowing a hunting horn. Another told him what it was like to bayonet a man in the stomach – 'the Hun gave an enormous belch, blood poured from his mouth, then he jack-knifed and fell down'. A third friend, an officer in a Highland regiment, had found himself alone in a dugout with a German whom he dirked, and then spent half an hour bandaging. 'What a damn fool – he should have finished him off,' commented my father.

Outwardly at least, he seems to have been unshaken by the deaths of his comrades, making the occasional grim joke. Speaking of a red-headed Irish cousin who had transferred from the Irish Guards to the RFC and was shot down in France in 1915, he said long after, 'We called him "Blazes" and by God he ended in blazes.' But the death of Harold Freeman, formerly the squadron's bright light, upset him badly. Freeman, by now promoted to major, had been one of the few in Palestine to achieve his ambition of being sent to the Western Front, encouraging my father's own hopes. He was horrified when the news came, glad that he had not been present to watch his friend's final moments. Over half a century later, he was still talking about it, shortly before his own death.

Despite a fairly extensive search I have been unable to find any record of exactly how, where or when Freeman died. But in a letter of 1967 my father – at no time prone to exaggeration – states that Freeman attacked six enemy aircraft single-handed, accounting for four of them before being shot down in flames. Freeman is known to have been a superb pilot, courageous and daring, so my father's account certainly seems plausible. One cannot help wondering why so little notice was taken of what appears to have been a death worthy of a Victoria Cross. As it is, he was just another casualty, just another forgotten young man.

The Handley Page bomber flown by Biffy Borton from England to Egypt, photographed by WELS 'on day of arrival' according to a note written on the back – 29 August 1918. Allotted to the Australians of No. 1 Squadron, it was later sent to help Lawrence, deeply impressing his Arabs. A note on the back says that Ross Smith was in the pilot's seat when the photo was taken. (Author's collection)

Although Seward obviously did a good job at the School of Aeronautics, which satisfied his superiors (and earned him promotion), and while he realized that the school was making a most useful contribution to the war, he was thoroughly fed up at not being able to see action. He was further unsettled when he saw the big, twin-engined Handley Page bomber (with a wingspan of 100 ft) that Biffy Borton, by now a major-general, had flown from Manston aerodrome to Cairo at the end of July 1918 – a record-breaking flight. Geoffrey Salmond, with his usual bonhomie, arranged a well-attended and no doubt uproarious dinner in Cairo – presumably at Shepheard's – to celebrate the machine's arrival in the Middle East. Biffy wrote happily that 'practically the whole of my fellows from Palestine had managed to get away' to attend it.[3] My father was among the 'fellows from Palestine' at the dinner, and I still own a faded snap he took of the aircraft when it was at Heliopolis airport with Ross Smith in the pilot's cockpit.

He had at least one opportunity of visiting the front line in Palestine. Written on the back of a photograph taken amid lush vegetation is 'Me beside the River Jordan near Ghoraniye July 1918. This place was within range of the Turkish batteries which had destroyed the bridge, just visible, on the previous day.' The British had been trying to seize high ground in the vicinity, as part of a carefully planned scheme to make the enemy think that their next big offensive would come across the Jordan.

Convinced he had fully recovered his nerve, Seward pulled every string and wire that he could to be transferred to France. He knew exactly what he wanted to do when he got there. By the summer of 1918 the Independent Air Force of 'super Handley Pages' – even bigger than that flown by Biffy – were in action on the Western Front, and there was a plan to bomb Berlin. Four-engined, these leviathans carried thirty 250-pounders, with a crew of six who were trained in night flying. My father had been promised one, probably because he had a well-deserved reputation for being a superb pilot, although he never mentioned this. He was eager to have a chance of 'hitting back' and take revenge for the Zeppelin and Gotha bombing raids on Paris and London.

However, as he put it, 'The damn war finished too soon.'

Notes

1. Personal information from WELS to author.
2. 'Operations Record Book', p. 3.
3. Slater, *My Warrior Sons*, p. 195.

CHAPTER 16

PRELUDE TO ARMAGEDDON

**By Nebo's lonely mountain
On this side Jordan's wave,
In a vale in the land of Moab
There stands a lonely grave.**

Cecil Frances Alexander, 'The Burial of Moses'

For the first half of 1918 Allenby was unable to resume the offensive. Because of Germany's massive attacks in France during the spring and summer, too many of his experienced divisions had been transferred to the Western Front and their replacements needed a lengthy period of training. The Egyptian Expeditionary Force was reduced to mounting a few minor attacks, such as the capture of Jericho in February, although the Turks were finally driven over the Jordan. During the next few months what action there was in the Jordan Valley consisted of raids eastward, across the river.

On 1 March Falkenhayn was replaced by General Otto Liman von Sanders Pasha, the former head of the German military mission at Constantinople, whose role in repulsing the Allies at Gallipoli had made him very popular with the Turks. A portly, red-faced, hot-tempered cavalry general, Liman was a rarity, a senior Prussian officer of Jewish descent. If not so gifted as Falkenhayn, he understood the Turkish soldier much better, realizing that his talent lay in dogged defence rather than subtle manoeuvring. But, outnumbered and under-supplied, he had a hopeless task.

Sefton Brancker had been recalled to London in January, to take up an important post at the new Air Ministry, and Salmond returned. Both of them ensured that the British aircraft did not remain inactive during the lull. In the last fortnight of January the Australian observers of No. 1 Squadron photographed 624 square miles of territory – 'with fine efficiency'.[1] The difficult, hilly terrain, honeycombed with wadis and nullahs, made their work particularly useful. In February a flight of machines from No. 14 Squadron was moved to Jerusalem to help with the limited offensives that took place before the bad weather cleared. Such mountainous country was exceptionally

General Otto Liman von Sanders Pasha, formerly head of the German Military Mission to Constantinople, who replaced Falkenhayn in March 1918. If not so clever as his predecessor, Liman was genuinely liked by the Turks and they worked well with him despite his impatience and hot temper. Hopelessly outnumbered, he did his best but proved to be no match for Allenby. (TopFoto)

dangerous in the dense mist. One aircraft lost its bearings and flew straight into a hillside – 'Pilot, observer and machine were an unrecognisable mess', recorded the war diary.[2]

The Huns were active, too, operating from their aerodromes at Jenin and El Affule, but 'Brisfits' never had any qualms about taking on double their number, always emerging victorious. After one such duel, writes Cutlack, when an Albatros had been chased down and landed on its back, 'The Australians waited till the pilot crawled out of the wreckage, and then chased him to cover with sprays of bullets.'[3] Even so, German reconnaissance machines bravely did their best to help the Turkish artillery.

On 27 March 1918, during an attempt to intercept one of these reconnaissance planes, which had appeared over his aerodrome at breakfast time, and accompanied by another scout, the Australian Captain R. M. Drummond of the new No. 111 Squadron, flying a Nieuport, suddenly found himself being attacked by half a dozen enemy aircraft. He later recounted the experience in an interview with Australian press:

> My mate [who] did not see them, followed the first machine down, and went off in ignorance of the danger. I had a stiff fight with the six new enemy scouts, shot down one for certain, and sent another down in a spin. But the remaining four were making the fight too hot,

and attacked me from underneath, where I could not get at them with my gun. They forced me down lower and lower, my engine was not working too well, and I was nearly done. I had had no breakfast – it is a bad thing to go up without breakfast. I dropped towards the enemy aerodrome in a spin, thinking I was beaten and it was better to be captured than killed.

I landed on their aerodrome, and some men came rushing out. Suddenly I found my engine picking up, and determined to give them another run for it. I took off from the ground and got about half-a-mile's start from the four Germans above, who had also concluded that the fight was over. I skimmed the hangars, and made for our lines. Here and there infantry tried to shoot at me. I was flying very low, only a few feet above the ground, and simply went straight at any men on the ground, and forced them to lie down. I landed four times altogether in Turkish territory – whenever my engine failed or a hill appeared – once in the middle of a cavalry camp at Mulebbis. Here they came up to take me again, and one fat man actually laid a hand on one of my wings, but again my engine picked up, and I fired a few more frantic shots and flew on skimming over their heads. I carried away a full line of washing as I left this camp. The four German machines kept on behind me and above me, but at last only one was left in the chase, and he, we found afterwards, was Felmy. I finally got home and landed just inside the Australian lines on the side of a hill. I fell unconscious when I got out of the machine – the evil effect of no breakfast.[4]

Few German airmen were taken prisoner. When (on the day of Drummond's adventure) a Bristol Fighter from No. 1 Squadron drove an enemy two-seater down near Amman, they machine-gunned it on the ground together with troops who tried to come to the crew's help, watching as their tracer bullets tore into the wrecked aircraft. 'Neither pilot nor observer were seen to leave the machine', said their report.[5]

There were a few lucky exceptions, such as Willi Hampel. Learning that he was in the prisoners' compound at Lydda, Alan Bott motored over and brought him back to lunch in the mess of No. 111 Squadron, showing him their planes, introducing him to the Squadron monkey and taking him for a swim in the sea, and then to tea with a German-Jewish lady at Jaffa.[6] Similarly, after Bott was himself captured, since he had been flying hatless and in shirt sleeves,

Oberleutnant Wollf – the man who shot him down – arranged for a brother officer from No. 111 to drop his uniform at a German landing ground near Tul Keram. Other Luftsreitskräfte officers made sure he received better treatment than usual at a succession of ghastly Turkish prisons, sending in hot meals from their mess. Even if both sides sometimes tried to obtain information from their prisoners, they preserved the fliers' code of chivalry.

By now, aircrew often found themselves living in delightful conditions, rejoicing in balmy weather. 'Our tents were pitched in an orange grove, which provided shade from the midday sun, privacy from the midnight pilfering of Bedouins, and loveliness at all times,' Bott recalled wistfully after his capture. He had been with a small group flying half a dozen Nieuports at an advance airstrip in a meadow near Jaffa. He remembered reaching out from his tent to pick newly ripe, giant Jaffa oranges and driving through the sand dunes for moonlight bathes in the Mediterranean.[7]

Jaffa (now Tel Aviv) photographed from the air by WELS, 1918. (Author's collection)

The war diary goes on to describe an attempt in April to assist the Arab Revolt.

> The advance of the Arab Hedjaz [*sic*] forces now made cooperation with them east of the Jordan possible. Amman, thirty miles as the crow flies, east of the Jordan, was the point selected for a raid. Near Amman the Hedjaz railway crosses a viaduct and passes through a tunnel. The destruction of these would seriously hamper the enemy and help the Arabs, and even if this could not be achieved, the destruction of the track for several miles would be a serious inconvenience to the Turk. A flight was dispatched from the squadron to Jericho to assist in these operations.
>
> The passage of the Jordan was first of all forced and the raiding troops advanced on Amman, seizing Shunet Nimrin, which covered the entrance to the Es Salt pass from which an attack could be made on the flank of our raid. The Jericho machines bombed Amman Station throughout the attack, destroying rolling stock and damaging buildings. Trains in motion were hit while a body of about one thousand [Turkish] troops in Amman were heavily bombed and attacked by machine-gun fire.
>
> Our troops on completing their raid once more withdrew to the west side of the Jordan, leaving strong detachments to hold bridgeheads east of the [river].[8]

This account in the war diary does not spell out the fact that the operation, which lasted from 21–29 March, had been a serious attempt to capture Amman and, by destroying the viaduct, wreck the Turkish railway system and cut off all enemy troops to the south. However, it ended in total failure because the Turks were still capable of putting up a stiff resistance. So was the Luftstreitkräfte, despite inferior machines. On 28 March 13 German planes caught and strafed the Camel Transport Corps at dusk at Shunet Nimrin, killing or wounding 175 camels, besides causing over 30 casualties among the drivers and the escorting troops.

The Luftstreitkräfte remained formidable. Early in April Captain Ross Smith reported that the new German base at Jenin, a double aerodrome, had been enlarged and now comprised 17 aircraft hangars and a hospital. He spotted 14 enemy machines on the ground, but there must have been more inside the hangars or away on patrol. Alan Bott was shot down the same month, jumped by three enemy scouts while pursuing a Rumpler, although it was the

WINGS OVER THE DESERT

Rumpler's observer that got him with a fluke burst of machine-gun fire from over 300 yards away – far outside the normal effective range.[9]

The war diary recorded a further attack:

> Another raid east of the Jordan was made at the end of April. Co-operation was arranged with the Beni Sakhr Arabs and an attack was made on Skunet while the cavalry, pushing round this position, seized Es Salt. As the Arabs failed to lend any support, we found it necessary to retire. Contact between the widely extended units engaged was throughout kept by squadron machines. Had we succeeded, the enemy would have been cut off from the east Jordan harvests.[10]

Again, the diarist minimises the failure of a minor but ambitious operation that lasted from 30 April until 4 May. It went wrong because the local Arabs, the Beni Sakhr, did not carry out their promise to cut enemy communications and Turkish reinforcements arrived swiftly. In any case, British planes had failed to discover extremely well-concealed Turkish positions in nullahs on the far bank of the Jordan.

On 1 May two aircraft from No. 1 Squadron did not return. Hit by Archie fire, one was forced to land near Amman, the crew burning the machine. Lieutenant Haig went down to pick them up but, while he was taking off, his undercarriage wheel broke and all three officers were taken prisoner. On the following day air-reconnaissance reports of the arrival of fresh Turkish troops made Allenby decide to break off the action. During the withdrawal a retreating column was machine-gunned by German planes, which by now was standard practice on both sides. 'Machine gun attacks upon Turkish ground-troops were first practised to any noticeable extent during the east-Jordan operations of March and April [1918]', Cutlack writes. 'They offered excellent fun for the airmen and wrought demoralising damage on infantry, cavalry, and transport alike.'[11]

Unable to resume a full-scale offensive, Allenby concentrated on training. For aircrew this included communication from planes in the air, using klaxon horns, Morse boards, lamps and flares. Even so, throughout the summer the enemy's positions were methodically bombed, aircraft diving down low on Turkish trenches. In the meantime, five more squadrons arrived. For reconnaissance, the BEs had been replaced by RE8s as well as by half a dozen Armstrong Whitworth FK8s which, if a bit clumsy, possessed a top speed of 104 mph. The scouts were SE5s or Nieuports. And there were more Bristol Fighters.

The turn of the tide in the air saw Gerhard Felmy's return to Germany in May 1918, probably because of ill health. (Cutlack records, wrongly, that he was killed at Damascus aerodrome while testing a new aircraft.)[12] A pilot whom both British and Australians regarded as their most formidable opponent, he was credited with four confirmed kills and one unconfirmed – four were necessary to qualify as an ace – while his contribution to his comrades' morale must have been enormous. By all accounts he was what was known in the language of the time as a very gallant gentleman.[13]

The pick of the new British planes had been given to No. 1 Squadron, not just the Handley Page but every Bristol Fighter in Palestine – 18 in all. Someone very high up had decided that the Australians should have the best machines, presumably because he thought they made the best fighting pilots. It can only have been Allenby. One reason why he may have reached this decision was because so many of No. 1 Squadron had served in the Australian Light Horse for whom, as a cavalryman himself, he felt profound admiration. His decision was justified. 'During the three weeks preceding the attack only four enemy machines were able to cross our lines', noted the diarist of No. 14 Squadron.[14] Never lavish with compliments, Allenby was to tell No. 1 Squadron at a farewell parade in 1919, 'You gained us absolute supremacy in the air.'[15]

Notes

1. W. Raleigh and H. A. Jones, *The War in the Air*, Vol. V, p. 177.
2. 'Operations Record Book, No. 14 (Bombing) Squadron', p. 45.
3. F. M. Cutlack, 'The Australian Flying Corps', p. 123.
4. Drummond's story is reprinted in Cutlack, 'The Australian Flying Corps', pp. 90–1.
5. *Ibid.*, p. 111.
6. A. Bott, *Eastern Nights and Flights*, pp. 4–5.
7. Bott, *Eastern Nights and Flights*, pp. 3–4.
8. 'Operations Record Book', p. 46.
9. Bott, *Eastern Nights and Flights*, p. 8.
10. 'Operations Record Book', p. 47.
11. Cutlack, 'The Australian Flying Corps', p. 128.
12. *Ibid.*, p. 65.
13. Felmy rejoined the Luftwaffe in 1935, but, despite being promoted to Generalmajor, his later career was undistinguished, perhaps because his health had been wrecked on the Sinai Front. He died in 1955.
14. 'Operations Record Book', p. 49.
15. Cutlack, 'The Australian Flying Corps', p. 171.

CHAPTER 17

MEGIDDO

**This is the song of the Gun –
The muttering, stuttering gun.
The maddening, gladdening gun: –
That chuckles with evil glee
At the last, long dive of the Hun ...**

Captain Gordon Alchin, RFC, 'A Song of the Plane'

By autumn 1918, the last German offensives in France had been repulsed, while the major cities of Germany and Austro-Hungary were facing starvation. Although the Allies did not realize it, they had broken the Central Powers' ability to continue the war. Soon Bulgaria and Turkey would ask for an armistice, then the Austrian Empire would disintegrate, and finally an exhausted Germany would abandon the struggle.

Allenby was given the reinforcements he needed, well-fed, healthy troops. According to his own account, he mustered 57,000 rifles, 540 guns and 12,000 'sabres'. Changing its view of sabres as fancy weapons, the Australian Light Horse had asked to be equipped with them, realizing it would do away with the need to dismount and use the bayonet. 'Their training in the use of the sword and in shock tactics may have been slight, but the dash and spirit of cavalry was in their blood and upbringing,' commented Wavell.[1] The artillery was better than ever, and so were the tanks and armoured cars.

In contrast, Liman von Sanders had 32,000 diseased, starving, ragged infantry, 402 guns and 3,000 horsemen whose mounts could barely crawl. Admittedly, he had some superlative German units and excellent Austrian artillery, but too few. His locomotives were fuelled by olive wood or vine branches, his medical supplies non-existent. He could expect neither aid nor reinforcements from Constantinople where Enver Pasha's regime, dreaming of a new 'Pan-Turanian' empire in the Caucasus (momentarily surrendered by Bolshevik Russia), had lost interest in Palestine.

Having duped the enemy into believing he would strike in the Jordan Valley, Allenby concentrated his infantry on the coast, with his cavalry behind

Turks taken prisoner after one of Allenby's offensives – by now the quality and equipment of Turkish Army personnel was deteriorating rapidly, as can be seen from their clothing. German commanders tended to treat them as savages, which caused deep resentment and soured relations with Ottoman officers. (Author's collection)

them. He was able to hide his preparations for attack because fewer and fewer enemy aircraft were flying over his lines. Liman von Sanders recalled:

> Throughout the summer [of 1918] German air crew on the Sinai Front had a very difficult time. German planes simply could not fly or climb so fast as the new British machines. With very few exceptions, two consignments sent out to us as replacements proved useless, and our needs on the Western Front made further replacements out of the question. Between the spring and the autumn our excellent Luftstreitkräfte lost 59 pilots and observers. Patrolling British positions more or less ceased in September. As soon as a German plane appeared, it would be at once attacked by large formations that prevented any sort of reconnaissance.[2]

Brigadier Borton now had seven squadrons operating from three airfields (Ramleh, Junction Station and Sarona), with over 100 machines. In addition to the Bristol Fighters flown by the Australians, there were 21 SE5s. The odds were no longer against British airmen, as they had been only the previous summer.

Having enjoyed technical superiority in the air for so long in the Sinai, it was unnerving for Luftstreitkräfte pilots to find their aircraft out-flown and out-gunned by Bristol Fighters or SE5s. The latest types of German machine ceased to reach Palestine – matters might have been different had the enemy possessed Fokker DVIIs. At the same time, the Turkish supply lines were in chaos, so that not only fuel but dead or wounded aircrew were irreplaceable. The authors of *The War in the Air* described the situation:

> It would hardly be an exaggeration to say that the Bristol Fighters of the Australians kept the sky clear. Whether they were engaged on strategical reconnaissance, bombing attacks, or offensive patrols, the Australian flying officers never let pass an opportunity to seek out and fight enemy aircraft, usually pursuing their quarry to the ground where the destruction was often completed.[3]

Haifa photographed from the air by WELS, 26 September 1918. (Author's collection)

A Halberstadt CLIV. There may have been one or two of these formidable German two-seaters in Palestine in 1918. Pilot and observer sat in the same cockpit, the former armed with a 7.92 mm Spandau and the latter with a 7.92 mm Parabellum – note grenades for use against ground troops or balloons. Powered by a 160 hp Mercedes engine, the Halberstadt flew at up to 116 mph and could operate at over 20,000 feet, handling well as a scout, but was no match for Brisfits. (Philip Jarrett)

Cutlack has argued that the Germans had new machines that were as good as anything flown by the British and Australians. They included Pfalz and Albatros DVa scouts, AEG and Rumpler two-seaters, and possibly one or two Halberstadt CLIVs, all of which could fly nearly as fast as a Bristol Fighter. In Cutlack's view, the enemy airmen as a corps 'ignored the fighting maxim, "Never show tail to the enemy", and therein, as nearly as a single phrase will express it, lay the difference between the two flying services'.[4]

Yet, while the fliers of No. 1 Squadron may have been exceptionally skilled and courageous, the Bristol Fighter really was better than any German aircraft, its superiority demonstrated by the sheer number of enemy planes it destroyed. Technical disadvantage was what defeated the German airmen,

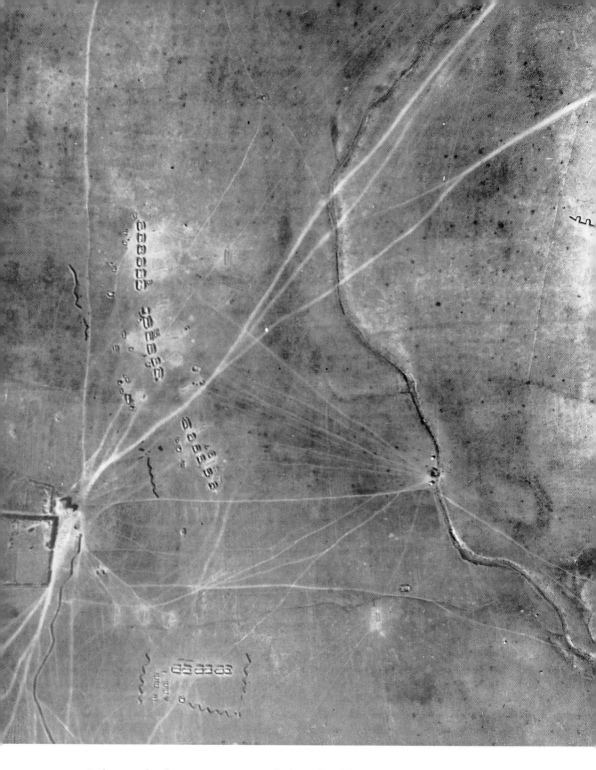

A photograph taken on 11 June 1918 during a bombing raid on Amman. (Author's collection)

The SE5 was a highly effective single-seat scout fighter armed with a synchronized Vickers gun firing through the propeller arc and a Lewis gun on the top plane. It was powered by a 200 hp Wolseley Viper engine and had a top speed of 138 mph – faster than any German machine. However, it only arrived in Palestine towards the end of the war. (Philip Jarrett)

not lack of fighting spirit. Besides combat casualties, many fell victim to local diseases – no medicine was available, while the Turkish hospitals, when they existed, were places of horror. (When a bullet was cut out of Falkenhayn's ADC, Rittmeister Krause, instead of being given an anaesthetic he was made to drink a bottle of cognac, an experience that put him off alcohol for life.)

In July Leutnant Hermann Kunz of Fliegerabteilung 301 shot down an SE5, but it was the last German victory in the air on the Palestine Front. Their pilots were further disheartened by complaints from the Turkish Army and growing animosity between German and Turkish officers.

In a single week in June, enemy aircraft managed to fly over British positions 100 times, but in the last week of August the figure dropped dramatically. The war diary tells us:

> During the three weeks preceding the attack, only four enemy machines
> were able to cross our lines. As a result, the enemy had no knowledge

of the new dispositions and concentrations made for attack. His papers, taken when the battle was over, showed complete ignorance of the vital changes which had been made. What attack he expected was east of the Jordan. He had no idea that every gun that could be spared from the eastern flank was unlimbered for action on the coast sector.'[5]

On 28 July two Bristol Fighters, piloted by Lieutenants Brown and Paul, pursued a Rumpler which they had intercepted while it was on reconnaissance, chasing it all the way from somewhere near Jerusalem to the Wadi Fara. The German plane's observer fought back with the utmost gallantry throughout the pursuit, exchanging shot for shot with the Australians, and his pilot managed to land safely in the wadi. However, 'Paul shot down pilot and observer as they ran from [the machine].'[6]

The strafing grew deadlier, more merciless. When a Bristol Fighter attacked a Turkish cavalry camp on the coast on 14 August, after shooting up the horse lines they machine-gunned over 300 Turks and their horses who were swimming in the sea. 'Despite much counter-fire from the cliffs, the airmen darted up and down the beach, pursued the bathers into the water or out of it into crevices in the cliff-side, and stampeded the horses along the shore', Cutlack writes.[7] Ten days later, another Bristol Fighter drove down a Pfalz, which it sent crashing into the side of a motor lorry. Miraculously, the pilot survived but, as he was trying to crawl out of the wreckage, his opponent finished him off with a single burst of gunfire.

On 27 August, when the big double aerodrome at Jenin was attacked it proved incapable of putting up any sort of resistance. Some pilots tried to take off but abandoned the attempt and ran for cover. The Brisfits were able to machine-gun the aircrews' tents without interruption. Again and again, German sources complain of a lack of pilots which made flying almost impossible despite the arrival of new machines. By now, their morale must have been on the verge of collapse – one can only guess at the frustration they suffered at their aircraft being unable to leave the ground.

Until mid-September, the situation was unchanged on Lawrence's front, although it was essential to cut the Dera–Damascus railway, the only line along which the Turks could receive reinforcements or try and escape. Since Dera was too far off to the east for Allenby's cavalry to reach quickly enough, he relied on Lawrence's Arab army to do the job. An attack was made on Dera station, its buildings and a large amount of rolling stock being seriously

A Bristol Fighter, armed with a Vickers gun firing through the propeller arc and two Lewis guns on a revolving Scarff ring for the observer behind. Fast and manoeuvrable, flown as a scout fighter it was superior to any enemy aircraft. After arriving in autumn 1917 the 'Brisfits' were crewed entirely by No. 1 Squadron AFC, who in 1918 drove the enemy out of the Palestine sky – German opponents called the plane the work of the Devil. The observer and pilot here are Lieutenant E. A. Mustard and Captain Ross Smith. (Philip Jarrett)

damaged, but the enemy put up a tough defence. Lawrence was unable to capture it, despite cutting the line in several places.

There were nine German machines at Dera – including a Pfalz and a 'yellow-bellied' Albatros, probably a DV – and it was they who kept the Arabs at bay. The one British aircraft available, a BE12 piloted by Lieutenant Junor, gallantly attacked the entire enemy flight single-handed – 'he suddenly sailed into the circus', says Lawrence, who continues, 'we again heard the drone of engines; and, to our astonishment, Junor reappeared, still alive, though attended on three sides by enemy machines, spitting bullets. He was twisting and slipping splendidly, firing back. Their very numbers hindered them but of course the affair could only have one ending.' Driven steadily lower, Junor ran out of petrol and was forced to land, his plane turning upside down. To everybody's amazement he emerged with only a cut on his chin, retrieving his two machine guns from the wreckage – a Vickers and a Lewis.[8]

The Arabs were terrified at being strafed from the sky, so Lawrence made his way to Allenby, explaining that the only enemy planes left seemed to be in his sector. In response, Salmond and Borton promised him that the Handley Page bomber would come to help as soon as possible. In the meantime, they sent two Bristol Fighters and a DH9 (a two-seater) from the Australian squadron, which, with Lawrence on board, joined the Arabs at Umtaiye. One of the pilots was Captain Ross Smith.

Next morning, their breakfast was interrupted by four German planes overhead and two of the Australian pilots raced to their machines, to intercept them. The third invited Lawrence to go up with him in the DH9 and act as his gunner. Lawrence (who writes so vividly that I make no apology for quoting from *Seven Pillars of Wisdom* at such length) takes up the story:

> I seemed not to understand him. Lewis guns, Scarff mountings, sights, rings which turned, vanes, knobs which rose and fell on swinging parallel bars; to shoot, one aimed with this side of the ring or with that, according to the varied speed and direction of oneself and the enemy ... No, I was not going up to air-fight, no matter what caste I lost with the pilot. He was an Australian, of a race delighting in additional risks ...
>
> There were one enemy two-seater and three scouts. Ross Smith fastened on the big one, and, after five minutes of sharp-machine-gun rattle, the German dived suddenly towards the railway line. As it flashed behind the low ridge, there broke out a pennon of smoke, and from its falling place a soft, dark cloud. An 'Ah' came from the Arabs about us. Five minutes later Ross Smith was back, and jumped gaily out of his machine, swearing that the Arab front was the place ...[9]

They had not yet finished breakfast when another German plane was spotted. Ross Smith's comrade from No. 1 Squadron, Captain Peters, immediately took up the other Bristol Fighter and soon shot it down in flames. 'Ross Smith wished he might stay for ever on this Arab front with an enemy every half-hour', Lawrence tells us.[10]

The arrival of the gigantic Handley Page (with Borton on board) at Um el Surab on 22 September awed the Arabs. Lawrence describes it being parked majestically, with the Bristol Fighters and DH9 like fledglings beneath its wings. 'Indeed and at last they have sent us THE aeroplane, of which these things were Foals', marvelled the tribesmen, who danced round the machine, singing, cheering and firing their rifles.[11] That evening it took off to bomb Dera, on the first of a series of nightly visitations.

In the meantime, Allenby had unleashed his autumn offensive, known as the Battle of Megiddo – a place once called Armageddon. Just before dawn on 19 September, piloted by Ross Smith the Handley Page bombed El Affule, putting out of action the enemy's central telegraph and telephone system on the coastal side of the front, beyond all hope of repair. At midday eight aircraft from a special bombing squadron did the same thing at Nablus, wrecking the Turks' communications centre on the eastern flank. In all sectors British planes systematically destroyed any means of signalling or sending orders, so that every enemy unit lost contact with headquarters.

'At dawn on September 19th the western mass attacked, rolling the Turks back north-east towards the hilly interior – like a door on its hinges', is how Liddell Hart summarises what took place that morning. Along the coast, British infantry smashed great gaps in the lines of the outnumbered enemy.

> Through the open doorway the cavalry passed, riding straight up the coastal corridor for thirty miles, before swinging east to bestride the Turkish rear. The only remaining way of retreat was eastwards across the Jordan and this was closed with shattering effect by the British air bombers. [12]

From dawn to dusk, scout machines flew above the enemy's aerodromes, strafing any attempt to get off the ground, so that no air information could reach enemy headquarters about the scale of the attack or from where it was coming. When the bombardment that opened the offensive had ceased – it lasted for only a quarter of an hour – other planes dropped smoke candles to screen the advance of the Allied troops. There was little if any opposition from the Luftstreitkräfte. The Bristol Fighters and the SE5s had finally driven their enemy out of the sky.

At dawn on 21 September the RAF located the Turkish Fourth Army and Seventh Army (the latter under Kemal Pasha, the future Ataturk), trying to flee through the gorge at the Wadi Fara. They had hoped to retreat to El Affule by way of Jenin but, realizing that El Affule was in British hands, they decided

The Bombing of the Wadi Fara, *20 September 1918.*
Mustafa Kemal's Seventh Army was spotted trying to
retreat along the narrow road through the long valley,
and the RAF and AFC bombed and machine-gunned
it for four hours, blocking its path with wrecked motor
lorries and wagons that made escape impossible. Many
aircrew were sickened by the butchery – the first occasion
when an army was destroyed by air power alone.
Painting by Stuart Reid. (Imperial War Museum
ART 3196)

to try and retreat by Nablus and Khirbet Ferweh towards Beisan. The attempt ended in horror. The war diary recorded the following:

> The enemy's line was stretched along a narrow and steeply winding road that threaded the mountain side, overhanging a deep chasm. It was difficult if not impossible, for troops caught here to scatter or take effective cover … From 8 a.m. until noon he was incessantly bombed and machine-gunned. Every two minutes two machines arrived over the column and every half hour an additional formation of six machines bombed and machine-gunned it … As a result of the bombing the road was completely blocked. Motor transport was blown across the road, wagons, horses, oxen, guns and limbers were an inextricable mess of ruin. In all, eighty-seven guns, fifty-four motor wagons, four motor cars and 932 wagons were destroyed or captured.[13]

During nearly 90 sorties, flying only a few feet above the enemy along a 5-mile length of road, pilots could see the massacre they were inflicting. Afterwards, Seward heard from his friends in No. 14 Squadron that many of them, some in tears, had begged not to be sent out to kill yet more Turks, but were ordered to take to the air again. He himself was shaken by their accounts. Biffy Borton was equally horrified. He wrote to his father, 'General Salmond who came up to stay with me went out to the scene next day, and was absolutely appalled at the havoc which could be produced by aircraft. WE ARE COMMONLY ALLUDED TO AS BUTCHERS.'[14]

There was almost as much mayhem everywhere else. On 22 September a DFW two-seater from Dera unwisely bombed Lawrence's encampment at Um el Surab, but was chased by a Bristol Fighter until it crashed, the pilot and observer being killed by machine-gun fire amid the wreckage. On the same day another Bristol Fighter bombed the aerodrome at Dera, destroying several machines on the ground, while during the night the Handley Page dropped a ton of bombs on the station. On 23 September the last serviceable DFW from Dera was forced down and bombed as soon as it landed.

On 25 September there was another large-scale massacre at Mafrak, where trains packed with Turkish troops were arriving from Amman in the vain hope of finding safety. Throughout the day British and Australian planes attacked the station here, shooting up the trains as they steamed in, firing almost 20,000 rounds of ammunition and dropping 4 tons of explosive. Over a thousand men must have been killed, while the fate of those who escaped was worse. 'Many

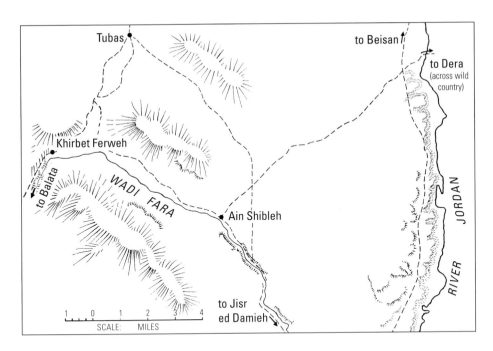

Map 4. The Wadi Fara where on 21 September 1918 the Turkish Seventh Army was wiped out by the RAF and the AFC.

Turks fled into the desert', is what Cutlack heard. 'The Arabs found some mad for want of water; others were never seen again.'[15]

The Fourth, Seventh and Eighth Turkish Armies had been annihilated. Meanwhile, the Desert Mounted Corps had galloped into Nazareth on 21 September, capturing the enemy's GHQ. Liman von Sanders got away only just in time. Followed by armoured cars, Major-General Chauvel's Australian cavalry then rode on to Damascus, which it occupied at about 6.30 a.m. on 1 October. An RFC friend of my father's, Lieutenant-Colonel A. H. Primrose, who took part in the ride (with a 'Popham Signalling Panel' for sending messages to planes in the air) told him afterwards that it had been 'a cavalryman's dream'. Fewer than 17,000 Turks escaped, with only 4,000 rifles between them.

The last flicker of resistance from the Luftstreitkräfte occurred at Muslimie Junction on 23 October when a Bristol Fighter forced down two DFWs onto the nearby aerodrome where, with four other German aircraft preparing to take off, they were destroyed by bombs and machine-gun fire. When British troops reached Rayak shortly after, they found 32 abandoned enemy planes on the airfield.

Because of overwhelming superiority in cavalry and aircraft, but also because of his genius as a strategist, Allenby had won what Liddell Hart called 'one of the most quickly decisive campaigns and one of the most completely decisive battles in all history'.[16] The forces of the Ottoman Empire in Palestine ceased to exist. Allenby had destroyed all three of the Turkish armies facing him, and captured 76,000 prisoners (including 4,000 Germans and Austrians) together with 360 guns. It was estimated that at least 10,000 of his opponents had been killed, probably far more, but not even an approximate figure is available. Allenby's own casualties amounted to just over 5,000 men, with fewer than 1,000 dead.

The Ottoman Empire agreed an armistice on 31 October 1918. Bulgaria had already signed one on 30 September, cutting Turkey off from its allies. Austria would capitulate on 4 November, followed seven days later by Germany. The First World War was over.

Seward was fond of recalling Armistice Night at Shepheard's Hotel. He said that full generals were doing somersaults in their boots and spurs on the main dining table, while the wretched manager was rolled up in the stair carpet. 'What did the manager think of it?' I asked him. 'How the hell should I know?' was his unfeeling reply.

Notes

  1. Wavell, *Allenby*, p. 259.
  2. O. Liman von Sanders, *Fünf Jahre Türkei*, p. 343.
  3. Raleigh and Jones, *The War in the Air*, Vol. VI, p. 208.
  4. Cutlack, 'The Australian Flying Corps', p. 112.
  5. 'Operations Record Book', p. 49.
  6. Cutlack, 'The Australian Flying Corps', p. 140.
  7. *Ibid.*, p. 143.
  8. Lawrence, *Seven Pillars of Wisdom*, pp. 616–17.
  9. *Ibid.*, p. 639.
 10. *Ibid.*, p. 640.
 11. *Ibid.*, p. 640.
 12. Liddell Hart, *A History of the World War*, p. 486.
 13. 'Operations Record Book', pp. 51–2.
 14. Slater, *My Warrior Sons*, p. 198.
 15. Cutlack, 'The Australian Flying Corps', p. 166.
 16. Liddell Hart, *A History of the World War*, p. 553.

CHAPTER 18

ON GEOFFREY SALMOND'S STAFF

For the past he buried brings
Back unburiable things

Rudyard Kipling, 'The Expert'

Early in 1919 my father was appointed a GSO 2 on the staff of Geoffrey Salmond, commanding the RAF in Egypt. Not only had Salmond moulded the shape of the air service in the Middle East during the war but he was credited with having assembled an unusually able team. Apparently the reason why Seward was chosen was his flair for organization. It meant there would be a future for him in the service, even in peacetime.

WELS at Alexandria as a GSO 2 on Geoffrey Salmond's staff, spring 1920 – a blurred photograph but a very good likeness. His rank badges are those of the RAF, while his cap and tunic are still khaki. (Author's collection)

Menu cover after the war was over, showing troops awaiting demobilisation – WELS is under the arch at top left, distinguishable by his broken nose. As a staff officer, one of his more unenviable jobs was to explain to mass parades why men could not go home sooner and that they must be patient. (Author's collection)

From the end of 1918 the staff had a new function, getting the troops back to Britain. Seward was given the task of visiting all aerodromes to lecture on the reasons why demobilization could not happen immediately. He was thankful he did not have to address the Australian Light Horse, ordered to slaughter their own mounts.

Social life in Cairo and Alexandria was hectic. There were plenty of interesting visitors from Europe, such as the young Lady Elizabeth Bowes-Lyon, with whom my father danced. The future Queen Mother had arrived at the end of the previous year and when, at a lunch party in 1998, someone asked her if she remembered her visit to Alexandria in 1919, she firmly corrected them, 'It was 1918.'

Some of Seward's friends were with the Interventionist forces fighting what he called the 'Bolos' in the Russian Civil War. He told me how when a flight of 'Big Acks' (Armstrong Whitworth FK8s) flew over Red Army lines on a bombing raid, 'a little bull-nosed Albatros flown by some renegade' came up in a vain attempt to drive them off. Next day, the hopelessly outdated plane did the same thing again, so it got shot down. He had no sympathy for the gallantry of the 'renegade' pilot, whose wife and children may well have been hostages for his behaviour in one of Trotsky's gulags. Other RAF friends were flying in Ireland. One of them, a Captain Gower whom my father had known in Wexford as a boy, bombed what he thought was a Sinn Féin rally but turned out to have been the wake of County Wicklow's most popular parish priest – Gower was rushed back to England that night. My father used to grin when telling this story. Even so, he was infuriated by reports of atrocities committed by the Black and Tans.

Two of his cousins who had served in the Aéronautique Militaire died just after the war. Prosaically if painfully, Gaston d'Ayguesvyves perished from Spanish flu. Released from his prisoner-of-war camp, the pioneer airman Pierre de Beausire-Seysell, whose example had first encouraged Seward's interest in flying, found he could not cope with civilian life and threw himself out of the window of a building in the Champs Elysées.

Meanwhile, the long-suffering Egyptians had grown angry at price rises and food shortages, especially in Cairo where the contrast with European luxury was most extreme. In addition, tens of thousands of *fellahin* had not enjoyed being press-ganged into the Egyptian Labour Corps. Ill-feeling was exacerbated by troops going on the rampage: the Australians were particularly disliked for their proneness to shoot up cafés or molest passers-by. And Egyptians deeply resented the fact that the martial law declared in 1916 seemed only to apply to themselves and never to foreigners. Their politicians dreamed of overthrowing what was a colonial regime in all but name, encouraged by the peace conference at Versailles insisting that every nation must become an independent country. Not until later did they appreciate that only European peoples counted as nations. Their leader, Said Zaghlul Pasha, would not accept that, having won an overwhelming victory, the British were in no mood to surrender the Suez Canal. He persisted, raising his compatriots' hopes to fever pitch. When he was arrested early in 1919 riots broke out everywhere, mobs murdering British soldiers, including several officers.

Russell Pasha, Cairo's amiable Chief of Police, was desperate to prevent a brutal response that might make the country ungovernable. However, Lieutenant-General Sir E. H. Bulfin, a hot-tempered Irish officer from the same mould as Dwyer of Amritsar, threatened that unless the riots stopped, troops would be turned loose with the bayonet on Egyptian areas of the city. When the news reached Westminster, horrified MPs made Bulfin withdraw his threat whereupon Cairo erupted. (This story seems to have been expunged from the history books.) Seward was in Shepheard's when it was besieged by an enormous crowd. Watching from the terrace, he saw two officers try to push their way through to the hotel. One was short and fat, the other tall and thin. The smaller was knocked to the ground and kicked to death, but the tall one pulled out a big automatic pistol and, firing into men's stomachs, shot his way to safety, leaving a trail of corpses.

My father kept his nerve throughout the unpleasantness. When a mob roared up the road to the main gate of Heliopolis aerodrome, he was waiting for them with a howitzer hidden under a tarpaulin: as they came within 50 yards he had the tarpaulin whipped off, whereupon they bolted, a round being fired over their heads as encouragement. Having promised to look after Stuart Reid's wife – he had been best man at their recent wedding – on hearing that she was staying in a 'picturesque' quarter of Cairo, far from the European area, he drove there immediately with a file of troops, and when Mrs Reid emerged, she was escorted to his lorry by fixed bayonets.

Even after Zaghlul was shipped off to Malta, Egypt remained a potential powder keg. Finally Allenby came up from Jerusalem and restored order. Zaghlul was released and a face-saving compromise negotiated, although Britain remained firmly in control of the country. However, the so-called 'Zaghlul Riots' disenchanted many Europeans, who ceased to regard Egypt as their home. The riots may have played their part in making my father decide to leave the service.[1]

He had been given a permanent commission in the new postwar Royal Air Force (one of only 600 out of a wartime strength of nearly 28,000 officers in 1918) and, for a major on the staff who got on well with his general, it offered a good career. Yet in the summer of 1920 he suddenly resigned his commission. A minor reason may have been that he lacked that mixture of flattery and back-stabbing intrigue that is needed for winning promotion in peacetime. Nor was he noted for tact – regularly voicing his opinion that Air Marshal Trenchard was 'a murderer', who had reached the top by sacrificing untrained pilots. He took a violent dislike to 'Jack' Slessor, a future air marshal, whom he saw as a scheming careerist. Neither did he have much time for another future air marshal, Arthur Tedder, whom he thought 'a colourless little fellow'. Even so, he was sorry to say goodbye to Geoffrey Salmond.

The real reason, however, was the traumatic toll taken on him by six major crashes. Rejecting seductive invitations to train the Japanese or the Bolivian air forces, he made up his mind to go back to civilian life. After he left the RAF, he only just declined a highly flattering personal appeal from Salmond to return to the service: having made arrangements to rejoin and even ordered a new uniform, he changed his mind at the very last minute.

My father sometimes described the 'Fourteen War' as his university. For a short time – a very short time – it even made him think of himself as wholly British, and from then on he talked and looked like a career British soldier, although the appearance was deceptive. He knew he was fortunate to have come through seemingly unscathed, while he was grateful for the challenges and the comradeship. The experience gave him enormous self-confidence, which, together with his natural vitality, produced something akin to real dynamism for years to come. Yet he had not been grounded for nothing. The psychological damage he had suffered was incurable and there was still a big bill to be paid. For over a decade, he did not realize that what he had been through would eventually make him unfit for a wholly normal existence.

Notes

1. For a balanced, objective account of the Zaghlul Riots, see P. J. Vatikiotis, *The History of Modern Egypt*.

THE DREAM

**I have a dream – a dreadful dream –
A dream that is never done.**

Rudyard Kipling, 'The Mother's Son'

Returning to England, Seward finished qualifying as a chartered accountant, without much enthusiasm. 'Wrapping a towel around my head', he was none the less able to do so within a few months, as he had already spent over two years in articles. Someone who always spoke of 'before 1914 when things were normal', he did not care for postwar London. In particular, he was shocked by what he regarded as the criminal lack of employment for men who came back to Lloyd George's 'land fit for heroes'.

While the English-speaking side of him remained more Irish than British, he did not like the look of Ireland either – at least one relative's house was burned down. He saw what was happening as a social rather than a national revolution, insisting that 'Anglo-Irish' was a matter of class, not of race or religion. (He would have been astounded to learn that this was a Marxist analysis.) He was laughed at for his ludicrous idea that Lloyd George's surrender to Irish extremism foreshadowed the end of the British Empire, even of the United Kingdom itself. Yet, despite his Unionist views, when he saw three Black and Tans drinking at the Trocadero Bar in London, he went up and kicked their table over – wisely, they declined to get up and fight.

There was no room for him in the family business at Bordeaux so, although determined that one day he would go back to France, in 1921 he found a job with the new Anglo-Czech Bank in the new country of Czechoslovakia. Among Montagu Norman's less-successful ventures, this was a bank that would end in failure. Even so, during his time with it my father acquired some colourful boon companions. Among them was Robert Bruce Lockhart (author of *Memoirs of a Secret Agent*), who introduced him to Prague's White Russian nightlife: they would spend from dusk to dawn listening to balalaikas, knocking back vodka, chatting to whores who had once been ladies and indulging in an occasional lovely rough-house, then return home for a bath before going sleepless to the office. He recovered by skiing in the Carpathians. Yet, despite the city's beauty, he always said he had 'a bitch of a time' in Prague, perhaps because he disliked the Czechs, whom he blamed for bringing down the Austrian Empire and whose patriotism he saw in the same light as Sinn Féin nationalism.

He was transferred to Vienna, where for a time he lived in a deserted cavalry barracks (the Rossauer Kaserne), acquiring right-wing cronies such as the Hungarian Major Fargo – optimistically plotting a Habsburg restoration – and Major Fey, the future Heimwehr strongman in Dolfüss's government, who was later murdered by the Nazis. He found time to play water polo for Paris against Berlin, half maiming an opponent who persisted in committing fouls – 'took all the skin off one side of his face'.

In 1923 he moved to Berlin as a chartered accountant for Binder Hamlyn. Here he grew very fond of Horcher's restaurant and also of the Adlon Hotel, in which he happily spent the worst weeks of the German inflation in a suite, drinking priceless hock and moselle. He recalled the 'Sylvester-Abend' (New Year's Eve) of that year as an especially cheerful occasion, with the hotel full of jolly young Hohenzollern princes. In 1925 he watched Field Marshal von Hindenburg, escorted by two squadrons of lancers, being driven into Berlin at breakneck speed to avoid being shot at by Communist marksmen, after he had been elected President. Suddenly, an airman (rumoured to be a Major Göring) flew down over the car, dropping what spectators thought was a bomb and making them run for cover, but the 'bomb' turned out to be a bunch of flowers.

On one occasion, he was introduced to the German premier, Gustav Stresemann, who impressed him, although he was convinced that Stresemann secretly intended Germany should one day go to war again. (In 1928 his friend Horace Findlayson, a counsellor at the British embassy, was sacked for suggesting that discrepancies in the German budget concealed expenditure on rearmament.) He also saw, close up, General Hans von Seeckt – the reorganizer of the German Army after 1920 – and noticed his odd combination of a Prussian officer's stern face with an artist's sensitive, even fluttering hands.

He met and liked Lord D'Abernon, the British ambassador. Because of his beard, D'Abernon bore a certain resemblance to Augustus John, whom he invited to Berlin to paint Lady D'Abernon's portrait. According to my father, in order to finish his picture John stayed behind in the embassy during the summer holiday while it was closed and was mistaken for the ambassador when, 'unconvincingly disguised in a beret', he brought back tarts whom he picked up in the Kurfurstendam – much to the scandal of Berliners.

One of Seward's new friends in Berlin was Fritz von Zellner, a former pilot in the Austro-Hungarian air force and one of the officers who had lined the streets of Vienna during the Emperor Franz Josef's funeral. When they met, Zellner had lost everything in the inflation and was sleeping rough on a bench in the Unter den Linden, where my father ran into him and, after a chat, decided to give him a job. Later, after again losing all he had during the second inflation, Zellner joined the SS. (In 1937 he would be good-natured enough to warn Seward not to revisit Germany because he was on a Gestapo blacklist.)

Quite apart from Zellner, my father always had some undeniably sinister friends, such as Karl Ibbetson, cashiered from the Danish Navy, and a French senator later rumoured to be a Nazi collaborator. The most colourful was a 'Red' Russian called Katya Krasina, whom I suspect must at some point have been his main mistress. She was one of the three beautiful daughters of the Krim Tatar Leonid Borisovich Krasin, an Old Bolshevik and early friend of Lenin, who suggested that his leader be embalmed and put on show in Red Square. Sent out of Petrograd to Stockholm in 1916 and educated at Cambridge during the 1920s, Katya lived on her wits in Paris with considerable elegance – deeply distrusted by the White Russian community.

During the 1920s my father's work took him to Munich, Cologne, Hamburg and Königsberg, to Brno, Budapest, Zagreb and Riga, accompanied by piles of leather luggage and a 'wardrobe' trunk – in the days when there was no air travel. He grew very fond of Dresden, where his mother settled for a time. Although he genuinely liked Germans and felt they had been badly treated after the war, he declined an invitation to represent the old RFC at Richthofen's reburial in Berlin.

He despised the Weimar Republic as feeble and degenerate, and the Nazis as 'gutter-snipes'. He first saw the stormtroopers at Mannheim in 1927, contemptuously recalling their shoddy brown uniforms and ramshackle lorries. Much to his amusement, his friend Wing Commander Christie (who ran MI6 in Germany) told him that Adolf Hitler was a carbon copy of Éamon de Valera. In his old-fashioned way he blamed republican France and the USA for preventing the restoration of the German monarchies – purged of Prussian dominance – since he thought this would have blocked the rise of Nazism.

Living abroad, Seward lost touch with his comrades from No. 14 Squadron. After being commissioned to paint seven paintings of the RFC and RAF in action on the Palestine Front for the Imperial War Museum, Stuart Reid settled in Australia where he prospered as a painter of race horses, dying in 1971. The gloomy Fred Minchin disappeared in 1927 while trying to fly the Atlantic. Another member of the squadron, Major Prout, who like Christie had joined MI6, killed himself at Bucharest with prussic acid after an unhappy affair with a Romanian lady. But, on visits to London, Seward sometimes bumped into Dixon-Spain, now a distinguished architect, who designed Newcastle City Hall, a hospital in Cairo, two churches and several cinemas – including one in Regent Street.

Seward spent his holidays skiing in the Alps, or in Italy as his mother had leased a villa on Capri, and added a working knowledge of Italian to his French, German and Arabic and smattering of Japanese. He also went down to Sicily, where he swam the Straits of Messina. His ambition, never fulfilled, was to divide his retirement between the Bay of Naples and the French countryside. In preparation, he negotiated the purchase of a château in the then remote Dordogne, the vineyards of which made it self-supporting, but abandoned the idea when his mother refused to live there and look after it.

In 1927 he was given the job of founding a branch of Timken, the American taper-bearing manufacturers, in France or Germany. Predictably, he chose France, establishing a factory at Agnières (later moved to Colmar). When setting up the company, he gave a lunch in London at the Savoy for Timken's American directors, and a friend offered to bring Winston Churchill to impress them. My father declined on being told that the great man would probably charge £500 for his presence, which was a hefty sum in those days.

For a time he achieved his ambition of living in what was his real homeland and the next years spent in his beloved Paris were the happiest of his entire life. As managing director of Timken Français SA, he was a rich man with a handsome apartment in the rue de Longchamps and a Bugatti – later exchanged for a specially built Hotchkiss. He saw a lot of the cousinhood, and shared their contempt for the politicians of the 'Salle Époque', whom he regarded as corrupt mediocrities who would never have made their mark in any other profession. Even so, he seriously contemplated becoming a French citizen. This existence was interrupted from time to time by business trips to the USA on board the great Atlantic liners, dining at the captain's table. Always staying at the St Regis, he learned to love the New York of prohibition and Eddy Cantor, recalling that 'the easiest way of finding a speak-easy was to ask what they call a "cop"'.

In 1932 he married, not a Frenchwoman but a very pretty and unshakeably loyal Irish girl 20 years younger than himself, although she possessed a mordant sense of humour he did not share. It was a surprising choice, as he had wanted his children to have French nationality, but the marriage was a happy one. In no way deterred by his ugliness, after seeing *La Grande Illusion* a few years later she joked that he reminded her of Erich von Stroheim ('the man you love to hate') in the role of Captain von Rauffenstein. Despite his ruined features, he cut an oddly impressive figure: as his admiring cook commented, *'Monsieur a la beauté de la force'*, much to his wife's joy. What struck her most were the many countries he knew and the strange people he had met. She found him fascinating, when persuaded to talk. A fluent French-speaker – after several years with the Sacré Coeur nuns at Brussels – eventually she became almost as fanatical a Francophile as her husband.

A little tactlessly, he paid his former 'friend' Katya to spend several weeks in showing her Paris while he was at his office, providing a car and chauffeur. The situation amused his cynical young wife, even if sometimes she did not agree with her guide and adored her new cousins whom Katya, as the daughter of a Bolshevik, called 'those stuffy old royalists'. Yet she always spoke affectionately of Katya.

Ousted from the Timken Company – as usual, he had made enemies – he and his wife moved from the rue de Longchamps (with his pre-Phylloxera claret, Caruso records and indispensable volumes of the Greek and Latin classics) to the boulevard Péreire. Here he lived in a service flat opposite Marlene Dietrich and her cameraman husband, Joseph Sternberg. (He was surprised by her speaking 'quite good French' and wearing a dinner jacket.) While he was in the boulevard Péreire his son was born. In 1936 he took his little family to Bucharest as a financial adviser to the oil company Steaua Romania, with the task of helping it smuggle profits out of the country in the teeth of King Carol's moratorium – and only just avoiding arrest in the process.

He was preparing to take up a job in Constantinople when he suffered a mysterious collapse, never properly diagnosed, one of the symptoms of which was a mild form of epilepsy that included frothing at the mouth. The legacy of what had happened to him during the war had left him a broken man. He once let slip that he had even been too frightened to go 'outside' (on top) on an unroofed London bus, while he refused to travel by plane. Any film with an air crash gave him nightmares: after a visit to a cinema showing a film of this sort, he was found bellowing in his sleep, holding his arms over his face. The dream never left him, recurring again and again. Although to some extent he recovered, his drive abandoned him, together with his money, so that he was forced to live on a tenth of his former income. He should have inherited the last fragments of the little Irish estate from his grandfather, once 1,700 acres of good farmland, but they had been sold off by an incapable uncle.

During the Second World War, instead of rejoining the RAF he worked in an obscure job at the Air Ministry. When war broke out, his wife urged him to go back, convinced that his experience as a staff officer would be useful. But he could not overcome his fear of having to fly. He bitterly regretted not being able to fight when he heard of the fall of France, which caused him terrible anguish; he blamed it on 'those gutter politicians'.

Apart from fear of flying, his courage remained unimpaired. Inhabiting a top-floor flat in London during the Blitz, he refused to go down to an air-raid shelter, preferring a quick death to 'being drowned like a rat in a hole', as he was convinced that any shelter would be flooded by burst waterpipes. He and my mother showed no emotion throughout the noisiest air raid, so that as a small child I was never scared by the sound of bombs. I simply didn't know what it meant, even when a charwoman started screaming. Dozing under a skylight one day, I was woken by a piercing whistle from a bomb that grew louder and louder as it came nearer and nearer; suddenly my father rushed into the room and threw himself over me – seconds later, the skylight shattered. Covered in broken glass, he stood up and asked if I would care for some lemonade.

In other ways, too, a little of the old spirit lingered, especially that ungovernable temper. His brother-in-law, stationed at Cairo during the war, told me that local cab drivers tended to overcharge; one morning, the police found the body of a driver who had been knocked unconscious and then had his own taxi driven over him. 'I couldn't help wondering if Eric had rejoined the forces and was back in Egypt,' joked my uncle.

His later years were especially sad and frustrating, almost his only friends being his wife and son. He even cut himself off from his French kindred, many of whom assumed that he had been killed during the Second World War. Aware that something inside him had snapped, although never complaining, he was so unhappy that it is surprising he lived for so long. His main solace was rereading his favourite authors, especially Plutarch, while he became a devout Catholic, reverting to the austere faith of his childhood.

Perhaps my portrait has been a bit too grim. If he was undeniably a strange and difficult man, it is only fair to say that his family were devoted to him. He could be extraordinarily generous: when short of money himself, he once handed over all the cash he could lay his hands on to a friend who had been made bankrupt. I don't think he ever told a serious lie in his life, while he was incapable of boasting. Despite that volcanic temper, he could be marvellous company. When I was a boy, besides trying (unsuccessfully) to teach me how to throw knives and to fence, he introduced me to Livy, the stranger novels of Alexandre Dumas père, the forgotten Irish romances of Charles Lever, to *bel canto* and the operettas of Offenbach. When I grew up, often he behaved more like a brother than a father. I owe to him my passion for history and love for a long dead France.

By the time he died in 1975, he had lost his mind. To some degree this must have been due to the damage suffered in the war of over half a century before; the dream recurred, if less frequently, until the very end. But when two youths tried to mug him during his senile eighties, they were seen running away with blood on their faces – the fierce old man had used his umbrella as an épée. He spent his last weeks in a lunatic asylum. One of his hallucinations was that he was a prisoner of the Turks; he insisted on speaking German, as 'those fellows understand it better than English'. While he was dying, a crazy old woman in the next room sang 'Roses are blooming in Picardy', over and over again. Somehow, it seemed oddly fitting, even though he had never served on the Western Front.

Right: *WELS in 1961, aged 70, with his battered nose – bloody but unbowed, and still as aggressive as ever.* (Author's collection)

A LAMENT.

(*Some way after Byron*).

———

Ten little bumble bees taking off in line,
    One hit a sycamore and then there were
       nine.

Nine little bumble bees flying fast and straight;
    One got a nasty bump and then there were
       eight.

Eight little bumble bees climbing up to heav'n;
    One struck an Archibald and then there
       were seven.

Seven little bumble bees attacking in a dive;
    One met another one and then there were
       five.

Five little bumble bees way above the floor;
    One saw the Hun machine and then there
       were four.

Four little bumble bees fighting fast and free ;
    One said his engine corked and then there
       were three.

Three little bumble bees scrapping in the blue;
    One came all over queer and then there were
       two.

Two little bumble bees hiding in the sun;
    One had a cross-feed jam and then there
       was one.

One little bumble bee faint but still pursuing ;
    He hasn't come back yet—nothing further
       doing.

                  D. O'D.

Every RFC pilot knew he stood a good chance of being killed – generally burned alive – so this defiant bit of doggerel made uncomfortable reading. The machines shown at the top are DH2 scouts, which reached the Sinai Front during the summer of 1917. From The Gnome, *August 1917. (Author's collection)*

CHRONOLOGY

1914

5 November   Turkey declares war on Great Britain, proclaiming a *jihad*.

1915

3 February   Failure of the Turkish attack on the Suez Canal.

1916

10 March   General Sir Archibald Murray becomes C-in-C, Egypt.
March   Arrival of No. 14 Squadron, Royal Flying Corps, in Egypt.
March   Arrival of Fliegerabteilung 300 at El Arish and Beersheba.
April   Arrival of No. 1 Squadron, Australian Flying Corps, in Egypt.
5 June   Hussein ibn Ali, Sherif of Mecca, begins the Arab revolt against Turkey.
3–5 Aug   Battle of Romani in northern Sinai – Turkish counter-attack repulsed.
November   No. 14 Squadron sends a flight to Yenbo to help T. E. Lawrence.
21 December   British occupy El Arish, unopposed.
23 December   Magdhaba captured by Anzac Mounted Division.

1917

9 January   Rafa captured by Anzacs – Sinai cleared of enemy troops.
January   No. 14 Squadron and No. 1 Squadron move to Kilo 143 at Ujret el Zol.
26 March   First Battle of Gaza – British repulse.
17–19 April   Second Battle of Gaza – British repulse.
28 June   General Sir Edmund Allenby replaces General Murray as C-in-C.
October   Arrival in Palestine of the first Bristol Fighters.
28 Oct–7 Nov   Third Battle of Gaza – Turkish rout.
7 December   Capture of Jerusalem.

1918

21 February   Capture of Jericho.
30 April   Failure of British attempt to capture Amman.
18 Sept   Megiddo offensive opens, ending in total defeat of three Turkish armies.
21 Sept   Bombing of Wadi Fara – first destruction of an army by air power alone.
30 Sept   Bulgaria agrees an armistice – Turkey cut off from Germany and Austria.
1 October   Australian Light Horse occupy Damascus.
23 October   Last German aircraft in Palestine and Syria driven out of the sky.
31 October   Turkey agrees an armistice.
4 November   Austria agrees an armistice.
11 November   Germany agrees an armistice.

SOURCES

Primary

Aaronson, A., *With the Turks in Palestine*, London, Constable, 1917

'Advance of the Egyptian Expeditionary Force, July 1917–October 1918', *Palestine News*, Cairo, 1919

Anon, 'Operations Record Book, No. 14 (Bombing) Squadron', AIR 27/191, Department of Public Records, Kew

Atkinson, C. T., 'General Liman von Sanders on His Experiences in Palestine', *Army Quarterly*, Vol. III, No. 2, London, January 1922

Bott, A., *Eastern Nights and Flights*, Edinburgh and London, William Blackwood, 1920

Cutlack, F. M., 'The Australian Flying Corps in the western and eastern theatres of war, 1914–1918', in *Official History of Australia in the War of 1914–1918*, Vol. VIII, Sydney, Angus & Robertson, 1923

Falls, C., *Military Operations: Egypt and Palestine. To June, 1917, and from June, 1917*, London, HM Stationery Office, n.d.

——, *The First World War*, London, Longman, 1960

Gullet, H. S., *The Australian Imperial Force in Sinai and Palestine, 1914–1918*, Sydney, Angus & Robertson, 1940

Joubert de la Ferté, P. B., *The Third Service*, London, Thames & Hudson, 1955

Kress von Kressenstein, F. Freiherr, *Zwischen Kaukasus und Sinai: Jahrbuch des Bundes der Asienkämpfer*, 3 vols, Berlin, Deutsche Buchandlung Mulzer und Cleemann, 1921–3

——, *Mit den Turken zum SuezKanal*, Berlin, Otto Schlegel, 1938

Lawrence, T. E., *Revolt in the Desert*, London, Jonathan Cape, 1926

——, *Seven Pillars of Wisdom*, London, Jonathan Cape, 1946

Lee, Lieutenant A. S. G., *No Parachute: A Fighter Pilot in World War I – Letters Written in 1917*, London, Jarrolds, 1968

Lewis, C., *Sagittarius Rising*, London, Peter Davies, 1936

Liman von Sanders, O., *Fünf Jahre Türkei*, Berlin, Scherl, 1920

Macmillan, N., *Sir Sefton Brancker*, London, Heinemann, 1935

MacMunn, Sir George, and Falls, C., *Military Operations Egypt & Palestine*, 5 vols, London, HMSO, 1928

Massey, W. T., *Allenby's Final Triumph*, London, Constable, 1920

Murray, A., *The Dispatches of General Sir Archibald Murray, June 1916–June 1920*, London, J. M. Dent, 1920

Pott, A. J., *People of the Book*, London, Blackwood, 1932

Raleigh, W., and Jones, H. A., *The War in the Air: Being the story of the part played in the Great War by the Royal Air Force*, 7 vols, Oxford, Clarendon Press, 1922–37

Reid, F., *The Fighting Cameliers*, Sydney, Angus & Robertson, 1934

Slater, J. (ed.), *My Warrior Sons: The Borton Family Diaries*, London, Peter Davies, 1973

Slessor, Sir John, *The Central Blue*, London, Cassell, 1968

Storrs, Sir Ronald, *Orientations*, London, Ivor Nicholson & Watson, 1937

Thomas, L., *With Lawrence in Arabia*, London, Hutchinson, n.d.

Tilière, Comte M. de, *Les heures de la Patrie*, St Lô, n.d.

Wavell, Colonel A. P., *The Palestine Campaigns*, London, Constable, 1928

Williamson, H. J., *The Roll of Honour RFC and RAF for the Great War 1914–1918*, Dallington, East Sussex, Naval and Military Press, 1992

Secondary

Baker, A., *From Biplane to Spitfire: The Life of Air Chief Marshal Sir Geoffrey Salmond*, Barnsley, Pen & Sword, 2003

Bruce, J. M., *British Aeroplanes, 1914–18*, London, Putnam, 1957

Buchan, J., *Greenmantle*, London, Hodder & Stoughton, 1916

——, *Memory Holds the Door*, London, Hodder & Stoughton, 1954

——, *A History of the First World War*, Moffat, Lochar, 1991

Bullock, D. L., *Allenby's War: The Palestine–Arabian Campaigns 1916–1918*, London, Blandford Press, 1988

Crutwell, C. R. M. F., *A History of the Great War 1914–1918*, Oxford, Clarendon Press, 1934

Dane, E., *The British Campaign in the Near East*, London, Hodder & Stoughton, 1918

Falls, C., 'Falkenhayn in Syria', *Edinburgh Review*, Vol. 250, Edinburgh, October 1929

——, *The First World War*, London, Longmans, 1960

——, *Armageddon*, London, Weidenfeld & Nicolson, 1964

Lewis, C., *Farewell to Wings*, London, Triumph Press, 1964

Liddell Hart, Sir Basil, *A History of the World War, 1914–1918*, London, Faber & Faber, 1934

——, *T. E. Lawrence in Arabia and After*, London, Jonathan Cape, 1934

——, *T. E. Lawrence to His Biographer*, London, Faber & Faber, 1938

Nelson, N., *Shepheard's Hotel*, London, Barrie & Rockcliff, 1960

Neumann, G. P., *Die deutschen Luftstreitkräfte im Weltkriege*, Berlin, Mittler, 1920

Norris, G., *The Royal Flying Corps: A History*, London, Muller, 1965

Probert, H. and Gilbert, M., *'128': The Story of the Royal Air Force Club*, London, privately printed, 2004

Vatikiotis, P. J., *The History of Modern Egypt*, London, Weidenfeld & Nicolson, 1991

Wavell, Field Marshal Lord, *Allenby: Soldier and Statesman*, London, Harrap, 1946

Wedgwood Benn, W., *In the Side Shows*, London, Hodder, 1919

INDEX